The Power of African Thinking

Leontine van Hooft

The Power of African Thinking

About **Ubuntu**, unifying leadership and a new world

Published by
GreenDreamWorks

The lettertype used in this book is the Ubuntu font. The Ubuntu font family is a free open source lettertype commissioned by Canonical, and released as 'Ubuntu Font Licence'. The lettertype consists of 1200 symbols, including Latin, Greek and Cyrillic letters. Enablement of the Hebrew and Arabic alphabets is in progress.

For acquisitions, please contact the marketing & communication department, GreenDreamCompany, Boschstraat 51, 5301 AB Zaltbommel, The Netherlands, Tel: 0031 418 517 435 or marketing@greendreamcompany.com

Translation: Alexandra King, Zaltbommel, The Netherlands
Graphic design: Foxy Design, Zaltbommel, The Netherlands

ISBN 978-90-820987-0-9
NUR 801

Follow us on

Contents

Preface

Among contemporary International Relations theorists, there is a school of thought that holds that a unipolar or bipolar world is more stable than a multipolar one, the latter being deemed anarchical. This theory is premised on the notion that concentration of power to one country or two, rather than a distribution of power among many smaller countries, makes for a more stable world as the unipolar world is likely to wield enough political, economic and cultural superiority to influence all others and none among the rest or no coalition can match the superior power. A bipolar world by the same line of thinking would create a constellation of satellite states aligning themselves with either power to create balance. There are enough theorists on both sides of the argument to create confusion. What is clear, though, is that the world today is poised at a critical juncture in history. Human civilization is at the crossroads of an era. Mankind is perched on the brink of a new world order and the branch of the fork we shall choose to take will determine an irreversible trajectory for mankind.

Following the demise of the Soviet Union in 1991, the illusion of peace that was to be ushered in by Pax-Americana, falsely believed to be a stable hegemon, has not held the world together. Neither has its capitalist model proved any less of an evil than the much-despised communist system that it so reviled and sought to replace. The deepening economic crisis that began in 2008 is putting into question the capitalist model, not to mention the polarity theory. The rise of China and other BRIC countries is causing much consternation in the current less-than-perfect global order. Are we headed for an anarchical multipolar system?

Whether it is the failure of a lumbering unwilling hegemon or its capitalist system that has led us into the mire, that is inconsequential. The world has to marshal enough will to pull itself out of the mess.

For those who believe in the theory of evolution and that man evolved from the spineless sea anemone to the homosapien species we know ourselves to be, I would argue that while the same evolutionary marvel that worked wonders to grow a spine, seems to have failed to develop the brain to elevate the human being beyond his base desires for materialism. Well, it would appear that debunking two well known (and perhaps loved) theories in one swoop is a huge risk.

While international travel has made far off places on the planet appear awfully closer, great strides in Information Technology innovations made the world ever so interconnected, and many cultures have interfaced and intermingled more than at any other time in recorded history, this has in reality, sadly, not resulted in commensurate tolerance and understanding among these cultures.

On the contrary, the world has lost its way and needs a new think and a new direction. One asks oneself: is there perhaps another way? I believe that the world is saturated with a multitude of brilliant ideas, most of them hiding in plain sight. Ubuntu is one of them!

Much in the West has been lost in the rush to attain full development. The so-called developed world has had a lopsided success story, where economic development has been achieved at the expense of values and an erosion of traditional family/cultural norms. I strongly believe that through a collective cultural values basket, we can find a more humane way. We can recalibrate our moral values compass to face south for a change – the Ubuntu Way. The entire human experience stands to benefit from this re-definition of the most important values that benefit all creations and bring us closer to what we were created/meant to be: comfortable in our skins, in harmony with our fellow humans, other creatures and with nature.

Ubuntu is both a linguistic expression and a unifying cultural norm among many Bantu speaking African cultures. Linguistically, all Bantu speaking peoples share the word *Muntu* or *Mundu* to denote *person* or *human being.* From this root, springs the word *Ubuntu*, which simply put means human-ness. In Rwanda, Ubuntu is a rich word that has many associated deep meanings. But beyond its linguistic meaning lies a deeper attribute which touches on what human-ness means: it also has the same meaning as *humane.* As an attribute, it denotes generosity and a welcoming spirit: a call for people to treat each other as they like to be treated, for people to be their brothers' keeper.

For parts of the world where the value systems have been eroded, Ubuntu can inject a breath of fresh air. For my part of the world, a return to our old customs has served us in great stead in the last decade.

Africa is today clichéd as the last frontier, usually for its rich and abundant economic potential. Hardly anyone is looking at Africa for its commensurately rich cultural potential. Yet, Africa has been a rising star in the last decade and the world is only now beginning to take note. The World Bank recently noted that six of the ten fastest growing economies of the last decade (2000-2010) were in Africa. Finally good news is trickling out of the "dark continent". The world is relooking at Africa, the cradle of mankind, with new eyes. It is the only continent with abundant resources and an abundance of growth and development potential.

In my own country, Rwanda, we have adopted a new thinking where we use our own homegrown and cultural best practices to solve problems. Gacaca, Girinka, Umuganda, Agaciro – all are old norms that have been revived as national programs to help us solve our problems. Rwanda has done remarkable work and we have been recognized worldwide for our unique "innovations" and tireless efforts to rebuild our nation. In just 18 years after a major traumatic event of cataclysmic proportions, Rwanda has established peace and stability within its borders and experienced remarkable social transformation, as well as astounding economic growth and development. Drawing on cultural practices and home-grown solutions, Rwanda has created new models for reconciliation and peaceful coexistence. One of the more known home grown solutions is the Gacaca traditional court system. But there are other less known socio-cultural norms at play, such as Ubupfura (nobility), that make Rwanda a truly unique country. All or some of these norms can be shared to make the world a more tolerant place.

The West is often at once condescending, contemptuous and dismissive about Africa, and seems to suffer from a "can anything good come from Africa" syndrome. You see this in the skewed media coverage, in the trade relations, in the parochial attitudes and in a variety of other ways.

No doubt, the West has reached a level of saturated development, where the only way forward seems to be downward. The West has a choice, to choose the more humane way, employing a combination of cultural norms from without, to complement its scientific and cultural innovation to create a better world. But it can of course elect to ignore the rest of the world and play brinkmanship and rush toward self-annihilation.

In a little anecdote in the Bible: when Philip found Nathanael, he told him: "We have found the one Moses wrote about in the Law, and about whom the prophets also wrote – Jesus of Nazareth, the son of Joseph." "Nazareth!" exclaimed Nathanael incongruously. "Can anything good come from Nazareth?" "Come and see for yourself", Philip replied.

H.E. Mrs. Immaculee Uwanyiligira
Ambassador of Rwanda

The Embassy of the Republic of Rwanda in The Hague is accredited to the Netherlands, Croatia, Estonia, Latvia, Lithuania and Slovenia.

From my desk

Around fifteen years ago, I began to spread my wings. With all the knowledge I had gained, I chose to liberate myself. I enjoyed various positions in the welfare and reintegration sectors, as well as education and private sector participation. But curious as I always am, I decided it was time to move on. I became an independent consultant, specialising in diversity and integrity management, and I happily supported various authorities and business circles for many years.

I worked with many organisations and companies where I found that both people and opportunities were under utilised and neglected, and I tried to provide better structure for them. I worked as an independent consultant, interim manager, management coach and trainer, and (intercultural) mediator.

When I was 45, I felt it was time to formalise my knowledge and experience with a university qualification. This was a Masters degree in Corporate Anthropology at the University of Utrecht, The Netherlands. This extended what I knew about the function of organisational cultures.

My passionate curiosity about other cultures led me to Africa. I quickly realised that my image of Africa was not entirely accurate. I was angry with myself. Why does the continent attract so much biased attention? Why has the West been fooled? Certainly, there is poverty, but there is also something else: I see hope, passion and ambition, and a strong sense of connection and belonging between people. These are values that I also encountered later in many other African countries.

At that time, I was able to experience Africa's strength and resilience not only in international business, but also in building valuable friendships through hospitality. Even in conversations with taxi drivers, I discovered quite another Africa than had previously been promised to me. I had many questions . . . it strongly influenced my work, my life and humanity. But more than that: it showed me the real poverty of the western world. All this prompted me to write this book.

To enable my knowledge and experience to have more significance both for the continent and for myself, my partner and I started a business: GreenDreamCompany. The company focuses on developing tourist areas in emerging African markets. Tourism is responsible for most of the gross national product of these countries. It also generates many jobs and reinforces a positive image. Moreover, this sector is in its infancy in most African countries, so it was a logical step. My partner could realise his beautifully ecological ambitions, together with my dream of organising projects focused on managing diversity, integrity and capacity building. Africa revealed itself as a continent of stories, and our passion for natural and cultural heritage added an extra dimension.

While the West struggles with the global financial crisis, Africa is now looming large on the horizon. Many growth economies are on the African continent. How can this be happening only now, when the world is in turmoil?

This book gives you an impression of the complex 'zeitgeist' in which we are now living. You will become familiar with Ubuntu, the humanistic philosophy of life rooted in the genes of the African people. This is the Ubuntu philosophy as I have encountered and experienced from my background as an anthropologist and entrepreneur in these emerging countries. You will see the relationship between this philosophy and the blooming of the African Renaissance. The book also offers the West several pointers towards exploiting this philosophy. Africa does not own a patent on Ubuntu, and the African approach is not the only one suitable for these new times, but it is certainly an approach which offers opportunities.

You will meet inspirational leaders moulded by the philosophy in this book; old masters and contemporary leaders alike. You will learn about their motivations and gain insight into how they work. In this way, the book offers inspiration and lessons for leaders and managers of today and tomorrow, and above all inspiration for people looking for a different way of living and working.

It would not be a book about Africa if it did not contain any good stories. Many of these stories I have experienced for myself, others are recorded or borrowed.

A word of gratitude goes to Her Excellency Mrs. Immaculée Uwanyiligira, Ambassador of the Republic of Rwanda in the Netherlands, for the captivating discussions about how the power of Ubuntu has reunited her country and helped its rise. I had these conversations with her during our joint trade mission on a tour of Rwanda, the land of a thousand hills. I thank her for her personal preface to this book, which she granted me so spontaneously. I thank her for her friendship.

I would like to thank my family and friends, for their belief in our African Green Dreams, and their support as we embarked on yet another business trip. GreenDreamCompany is made possible through your firm support and has become a true family business. Please keep going, there is still much to do, and we cannot do without you.

But above all, my greatest thanks go to my 24-hour soul mate, Léon Rijckevorsel. He told me that it was time to write this book. As an entrepreneur / business partner and life companion he often gave me 'time off' to sit at my writer's desk. I thank him for his wisdom, feedback and all our African adventures. Long may we continue to do business together – with our minds, hearts and hands - in this beautiful continent!

I sincerely hope that this book may inspire you to approach the challenges of this global time. There are so many. They need your strength, commitment and passion.

I also hope that you will at least be somewhat surprised at Africa's potential. *With open eyes* . . . (Ethiopian proverb)

I sincerely hope that you too will wish to become acquainted with all this.

Leontine van Hooft MA
Zaltbommel, The Netherlands, October 2012.

The World Upside-Down

Again, you can't connect the dots looking forward; you can only connect them looking backwards. So you have to trust that the dots will somehow connect in your future. You have to trust in something - your gut, destiny, life, karma, whatever. This approach has never let me down, and it has made all the difference in my life.

Steve Jobs, 2005

You might say that there are plenty of signs that show that individualism and egocentrism have had their day. The twenty-first century citizen cries out for connection and demands a better world. This is shown in all sorts of civil movements, such as Occupy, The Tea Party, the Green Revolution, or the need for corporate social responsibility (CSR).

Just how complex is the twenty-first century in reality? What is being played out on the world's stage? Whose Golden Age will it become?

Many great changes are happening now, with no end in sight. It promises to be a captivating period, which demands proper leadership in the twenty-first century, in all its complexity and with its global questions.

The people's cry

You often hear people say that things should be different. People require that their surroundings, government and employers all deal differently with People, Planet and Profit. They ask this despite the crisis which mostly concerns the West, or perhaps precisely because of it, at the moment. A period of crisis can herald a call for change. The citizen can see a connection between every crisis at present: economic, environmental, climate and food. Apparently this is enough. We are now in the middle of a period of transition: the old and trusted capitalistic values within individualism are no longer sufficient – money is not an adequate motive any more – but we do not yet have any new values. We do not yet really know how to proceed. The citizen is increasingly searching for significance and connection, and looks at the context more effectively. IT plays a large role in this. The world has now become a village, where other norms and values become more accessible through Twitter and Youtube. In addition, we are also seeing a bewildering array of new economic and pro-change movements appearing both left and right in the fast lane of the world's stage. These influences affect citizens even further, as their worldview becomes shaken up and rapidly changed.

Of course, you could allow yourself to be continuously lead, as a citizen, through every example of crisis, negativity, intolerance and unrest in the western world. However, you could also exploit and confront the challenges afforded by this greatly changing world together, licking your wounds, setting the balance and determining a new course. Emerging freelancers who want to leave the rat race and change tack are all examples of citizens choosing change, no matter how testing this might be for them. It is now high time to wake up.

Hibernation is over; this is your wake up call

What exactly is going on during this period of transition? What are people's requirements, ambitions and interests in this confusing world? In order to answer this, it is important that we look back to when we could see the first signals of change.

The omens of the current changes were already visible halfway through the last century, particularly in the western world, in the shape of hippies and flower power. Who could forget the musical 'Hair', with its song 'The Age of Aquarius'? Or John Lennon's and Yoko Ono's 'War Is Over' campaign, or especially Martin Luther King's legendary speech: 'I have a dream . . .' This was the time that saw the rise of the New Age movement.

What did all these people and movements have in common with each other? They recognized in themselves a common factor, where they valued an intuitive and sensitive approach to problems and issues. They were big-hearted, with a highly developed feeling for justice. What they also shared was the loosening of

'I actually thought that it would be a little confusing during the same period of your life to be in one meeting when you're trying to make money, and then go to another meeting where you're giving it away.'

Bill Gates

the establishment, resisted by many young people and students. They called for worldwide peace, equality for men and women. They were against atomic energy, and wanted to be their own masters.

Initially, people thought this was only a temporary phenomenon, but it became gradually more apparent that it heralded things to come. The citizen would start to take more steps towards change during this new period. The doctor, the vicar and the lawyer were no longer sacrosanct. And the emergence of IT only strengthened this acquired independence.

However, we can see a yet more important development on the world stage. The power of multinationals and hugely wealthy leaders has become larger and more influential than governments and administrations during the last few decades. Rising economies see these multinationals and leaders more as catalysts and partners in the fight against poverty. It is no longer the traditional NGO's or religious foundations that seem placed to solve the poverty problem, but now we see new NGO's such as the Bill and Melissa Gates Foundation. They represent the new money, which can banish worldwide poverty and disease.

The majority of young people from the flower power era are facing a world far-removed from their former ideals.

Most of them are now over fifty-five years old. Some of them have acquired key positions in organizations or are at the helm. It seems that these people earning good money in this later phase of their lives, are now looking back to their youthful ideals, where they can use their skills, commercial talent and abilities to still accomplish these old ideals. They enjoy power and respect, and have great influence on the changing world stage. This influence had been reserved for the government, the church and traditional NGO's for decades. Now you can see more individuals who want to make their contribution to a better world – and you do not have to be as rich as Bill Gates.

The way back: from collectivism, individualism and egocentrism to solidarity

We have come a long way from our collective family culture to an individualistic culture. It has taken the western world fifty years to build a powerful, independent identity after the Second World War. This was a period where hard work went hand in hand with relative calm and stability. The western world became familiar with the concept of welfare. During this period, the government increasingly took the lead in many matters that families had previously arranged for themselves, for example care of the elderly and bringing up children. The government took over the family role, and family culture began to recede from us. Western culture was characterized by individualism, self-reliance and freedom, which became translated into life, living, work and education. This was reflected by material enrichment within the western free market economy.

After the attacks in the USA on 11 September 2001 (9/11), it became even more obvious that not everyone agreed with the individualistic development in the western world. The period of calm and an introspective attitude was definitely over; chaos reigned and the world tumbled into confusion. Blazing feelings of anger and uncertainty triggered by this lead to a hardening of attitudes, intolerance and inhospitality, and also to mistrust of the authorities.

It subsequently became even more painfully clear in 2008, that the enrichment of the financial world was beaten by the grab and bonus culture, which opened the floodgates with disastrous results. The world, which had become a global village because of IT possibilities, was a witness to this, not only in the West, but also further afield. Such conduct can have a great effect on people and their well-being. The beginning of the economic crisis in Wall Street immediately resulted in recession in Europe.

A culture of anxiety arose in the West because of this confusion and disorganisation. One striking detail in this is the deeply-held belief in the West that the economic crisis would affect the whole world. Nothing could be further from the truth. There are in fact many countries that are now experiencing the chance to rise out of a long period of poverty. In contrast to western culture, these countries, with their rich history and past experience of poverty, have a culture founded on hope and happiness, especially in difficult times.

The small mountain state of Bhutan offers particular and authentic wisdom. Since the seventies, 'gross national happiness' rather than 'gross national product', which can only lead to greed, has been central to this small Buddhist country. They have successfully translated this philosophy into their government. Their 'gross national happiness' can be measured by the amount of children playing freely in the streets.

In these uncertain times, people are searching for personal and spiritual refuge. At the same time, they are also searching for group identity. This comes from a need to belong to an association, and to measure virtual identity. Such groups offer certainty, and occupy a large part of today's society. Social media, like Facebook, Twitter and LinkedIn, enable people to connect with 'friends' all over the world and share positive messages. In addition, many books on the power of positive thinking are now appearing.

Migration, communication and modern tribalism

Today's politics seems to make us believe that immigration is a new phenomenon. This is certainly not the case. Jewish communities had already become established in Western Europe in the sixteenth century. Many other immigrants from former colonies have moved into Western Europe since then. Later still, other populations also moved, particularly from Northern Africa and Turkey. Opening the European borders has meant a wave of workers emigrating from Eastern Europe. At the same time, many Western Europeans left for countries such as Australia, New Zealand and Canada after the Second World War. Since then, many Dutch people have also established themselves as immigrants.

In contrast to earlier generations of immigrants, those of today are better able to simultaneously retain their cultural identity and find their place in a new fatherland. Immigrants can be from both Ghana and Amsterdam, and their very colour only adds to a city or organisation. They live in their own neighbourhoods, form associations and start their own local economy. The multicultural society, which we recognise in the Netherlands, is more of a 'salad bowl' than a 'melting pot'. As children of two cultures, these *diasporas* are very valuable to business transactions in the globalised world.

The information era, in which we now live, ensures that people know very well how to connect via the Internet and social media on a grand scale. This means that people from a similar culture, lifestyle or religion can easily communicate without meeting physically. They can therefore complete their connection very well. This offers great opportunities to widely-scattered diasporas from all over the world. We are now talking about *modern tribalism*.

In his book 'Here Comes Everybody', Clay Shirky writes about the tribal character of digital groupings, which show how communication, networks and organisations have definitely changed. These digital groupings can actually arise through social phenomena such as the Arab Spring protests, organised through Twitter. But we can also use Twitter for trivial events, such as an impromptu arrangement to meet for a drink in the pub.

The Macheta tribe, originally from South Africa, have spread worldwide, after finding each other via the Internet. Their members are unified in regaining the land taken from them through Apartheid. They are now successfully benefiting from the South African government's land reform bill.

One truely contemporary tribe is the Occupy movement. They protest about the banks' greed, which they see as the fundamental reason for the financial crisis. They act against world economic inequality with slogans such as 'We are the 99%' and 'Enough is enough', and they make full use of modern means of communication. This common objective unites people with diverse political beliefs and religions from all over the world.
Virtual networks like Facebook can also be identified as a modern tribe. This social network has developed into a meeting-place where allsorts of sub-tribes can arise from a common background or passion.

TED is a very powerful, modern tribe. It came into being in 1984(!) following a conference whose passionate goal was to bring three worlds together: Technology, Entertainment and Design. The promoters wanted to spread positive ideas worldwide through this means. It was such a success, that the TED website was transformed into a digital platform where interested parties from all over the world have access to the most inspirational speeches. Everyone can now enjoy the speakers 'live' on Youtube, and gain from their ideas and energy. Meanwhile, TED's motto, 'Ideas worth spreading' has now become 'Ideas worth doing'.

Modern tribes enable people to distinguish themselves from the masses. They are now searching for identity again in this period of individualism, crisis and spiritual poverty. They want to contribute, and feel good somehow. This need for connection is obviously so strong that many freelancers have joined modern tribes in all sorts of networks. They contact each other via LinkedIn and Facebook, making appointments and meetings at Open Coffees, Seats2meet, becoming increasingly jointly concerned with attractive industrial or green workspaces. Many new tribal partnerships emerge from these meetings.

Modern tribalism as a critical success factor within organisations

There have always been tribes. In an individual context, tribes can be experienced as oppressive, and belonging to former civilizations. But nothing could be further from the truth. It is generally agreed that this very need for solidarity lead to discovering how these ancient tribes functioned. The basis of successful tribal function is rooted in the fact that they developed a finely honed living and working society. They knew that fellowship and commitment lead to a collective enterprise, and therefore ensured their right to existence. This rationale is based on the certainty that people with a 'we' perspective participate more fully. And is that not what is needed today?

A strongly rooted tribal principle has contributed to rapid economic growth in African countries. Their challenge now is to retain their strong tribal mechanism and at the same time to enter into this modern world. This will help them learn a great deal from the lessons of the western world, whose individualistic society developed after the Second World War. They are also searching for a linking model.

In these times of austerity and clean-up measures, it still remains a big challenge for companies and organisations in the western world to create a 'we' perspective. Many of them are already trying to do this, through CSR responsibilities, for example, which show their world involvement. At the same time, socially responsible businesses show their true face to their clients. Because many organisations are still based only on economic laws and the strength of the most powerful, they miss many chances. It is astonishing that organisations and companies do not make more frequent use of modern tribalism. It may only occur to them sporadically that creating a tribe can increase the involvement of their clients, employees and others. Companies who do successfully practise this, often confine it in the western world to *tribal* marketing. This is how Apple built its community of products, services and innovation, by using marketing. This is a start, but there is much more to learn from modern tribalism. There are fortunately many companies and organisations, both on the African continent and in the western world, who are aware of using tribal mechanisms in their business operations and marketing strategies. They understand the importance of creating communities around their personnel, as well as their innovative products and services.

Beyond Maslow's pyramid

The universally acclaimed Maslow's pyramid, published by Abraham Maslow in 1943, shows a five-phase hierarchy of needs. Maslow describes these as organic or physical needs, for safety and certainty, solidarity, value, recognition and self-respect, and finally, self-realisation.

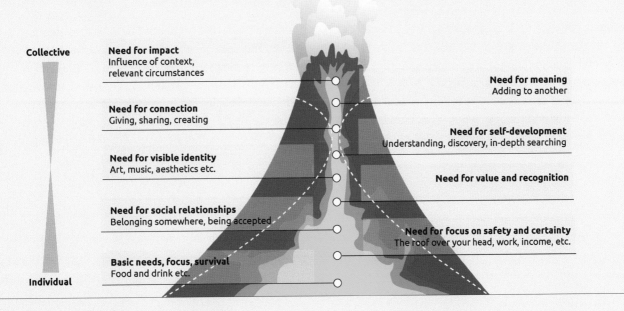

Collective

Need for impact
Influence of context, relevant circumstances

Need for connection
Giving, sharing, creating

Need for visible identity
Art, music, aesthetics etc.

Need for social relationships
Belonging somewhere, being accepted

Basic needs, focus, survival
Food and drink etc.

Individual

Need for meaning
Adding to another

Need for self-development
Understanding, discovery, in-depth searching

Need for value and recognition

Need for focus on safety and certainty
The roof over your head, work, income, etc.

The volcano model (Copyright Leontine van Hooft)

This model is strongly linked to an individual culture, and needs updating to the new collectivism in today's period of transition. Assuming that this new period is developing themes of giving meaning to others rather than to yourself, and mutual solidarity, this should mean that the individual transcends himself, as it were. The model may then 'erupt' around these themes, and become transformed into a volcano model.

A green engine for the well-being of the earth, people and the economy

Because the citizen thinks things must change, green economy now seems of great significance. The United Nations Environment Programme (UNEP) defines green economy as 'an economy that results in improved human well-being and social equity, while significantly reducing environmental risks and ecological scarcities'. This means in reality that whichever economic developments are necessary must be beneficial for people, nature and the environment. The basis of this green economy is clean and safe production of goods, materials and energy. It is also a circular economy – think about Cradle 2 Cradle, with its recycling and bio-degradability – with a desire to be independent of oil-producing countries.

Care of the earth and the well being of its population also provides scope for completely new industries to develop.

In fact, more responsible use and exploitation of the earth regarding business opportunities will lead to a better world.

Various tribal communities are again emerging from this green economy, who know how to put their own interpretation on it. Central to it are autonomy, happiness, self-realisation and experience. One example of this is Energie Dongen, a Dutch cooperative association amongst the inhabitants of Dongen, who want to realise their own affordable and sustainable energy together. Their mission is an energy-neutral Dongen. Members of the association are tenants, house owners, sports clubs, businesses and care institutions. These organisations function in the same way as tribal communities, and will become very important in the future. They are seriously taking up the fight against traditional organisations and markets in their ambitions to work towards a better world.

Western governments should be wise to giving free rein to this sort of reform and sustainable innovation. The choice made by governments to economise above substantial renewal brings us back to Maslow's individualistically tinted pyramid, while we have to make big strides forward. It is strange that western governments are more concerned with economising,

'Large-scale combinations of learning, working and business can emerge from new manufacturing industries, also cooperation between campuses, schools and businesses. This will provide massive work opportunities for the Netherlands (ten thousand jobs a year) economical and structural reinforcement, and lasting innovation.'
Jan Rotmans, Professor of Sustainability and Transition at the Erasmus University of Rotterdam, The Netherlands (2012)

with scarcely any attention to systematic renewal. They have restricted themselves to reforming the housing sector, healthcare and education, while they should be aiming for lasting innovation.

'There is no time or room for a rethink of our economic system when fundamental reform is now the only escape', according to Jan Rotmans

The Chinese are coming

Whilst the West is mostly in confusion, and diligently searching for solutions, China is ensuring great changes in our trusted world order at the moment. Where the West fears the advent of the Chinese, Africa is doing plenty of business with them, which means they are benefiting from the West's confusion and crisis. Meanwhile, seven out of ten of the world's growing economies come from the African continent. Africa is for the Chinese what China is for the West: somewhere with a great deal of cheap work potential, and above all, many clients.

This Chinese saying has literally brought the Chinese onto the African continent. They are building roads and laying rail tracks, which all contribute enormously to Africa's development. The Chinese presence shows that the western democratic model does not have to be a condition in the fight against poverty. Indeed, China has organised affordable loans for this work to be carried out. This shows that it is possible to collaborate economically without recourse to internal politics.

The Age of Aquarius, the Mayan Calendar and the power of the self-fulfilling prophecy

People's need for structural change, businesses looking for new organisational and earning models, connecting with the green economy, tribal groups who can contribute to a better world together, a shift of world-balance towards the arrival of new and large economies – these are all signs that we are entering into a new age, where an evolutionary process occurs in a different human consciousness. This will have logical consequences for the human mindset, for who does not wish to be part of a better world?

It is no coincidence, according to astrologists, that great changes are taking place in human consciousness right now. They attribute this to the sun, whose vernal equinox has shifted from the zodiac sign of Pisces to that of Aquarius, and say it is connected to human consciousness on earth. The process of the sun pushing us into a new age is automatically taking place. We do not need to do anything about this. The shift has various consequences, which are not linked to climate change. This New Age of Aquarius is destined to become a long period of peace, justice, respect and creativity. It is even supposed to be a new Age of Enlightenment.

The Mayan Calendar reaches the same conclusion. The Mayans were not aware of any lineal chronology, but saw time as a series of inter-linking circles. The new cycle was predicted to begin in 2012, and was characterised by wisdom, harmony, peace, love and the end of chaos. This would not be the end of the world, as many claimed, more that the world as we knew it was coming to an end. They called the previous era the fourth cycle, which combined masculine energy with water. The fifth Mayan cycle predicted a period of fusion between masculine and feminine energy. It would become a period of balance where these energies would once again be aware of, and a support to each other.

But even if astrologers look in a rather far-fetched way at the Age of Aquarius, or the Mayan's prophecies, it cannot be denied that there are cultures that bring about great social and economic changes on the basis of the self-fulfilling prophecy, particularly on the Asian and African continents. Ethiopia is a country which has its own calendar, based on the ancient Egyptian era. The Ethiopians celebrated the third millennium about seven years after the western world, namely on 12 September 2007. They gained an enormous amount of positive energy, because the population was so convinced that this millennium was related to the renaissance of such a powerful Coptic-Christian Ethiopia. Pride and hope in all levels of the population was translated into boundless energy and ambition. Here is a country tackling its greatest enemy, poverty, from within. The Ethiopians, with all due respect to their past, are striving to become a middle-income, or even a 'Zero CO2' emission country, instead of a low-income one, between now and 2020. The figures for the rising economy show that they are on schedule. It now relates to a very powerful mindset that calls for progress and enforces respect.

Because many people believe in the Age of Aquarius, the Mayan calendar or the self-fulfilling prophecy, or the advent of a hope-culture, there are now greater positive possibilities for us to call for a better world.
'You do not have to be an astrologer,' a Mayan or Helga van Leur (a well-known Dutch weather forecaster) to see that we are living in turbulent times. The planet earth is now concerned with renaissance. The evolution of human consciousness is, unfortunately, not unfolding automatically, or at the same tempo. We must pay attention to the needs, ambitions and concerns of people, if we are to stay within this period of transition. Visionary leadership is therefore indispensable.

Concluding remarks
What would happen if organisations recognised this period of transition, and further explored the possibilities of establishing a greener world? Maybe they would fulfill a pioneering role. This is something that seems to be working both in contemporary politics as well as religion. A very special kind of leadership is necessary to best anticipate and profit from it; not the sort of leadership at the root of the crisis, but rather leaders who know how to rise above their own importance. These leaders have the courage, audacity and the ambition to share with others at this complex time. The west needs some good, new role models if it wants to stay in the running, but in fact, such leaders are difficult to find.

Leaders With Courage, Vision, Passion and Compassion Wanted!

'If you want to build a ship, don't drum up the men to gather wood, divide the work and give orders. Instead, teach them to yearn for the vast and endless sea.'

Antoine de Saint-Exupéry, *La Citadelle*, 1948

The leaders who caused them cannot combat modern crises. They do not possess the required capacities, the appropriate mentality or the right character. Furthermore, they no longer enjoy the trust of the citizen. The complexity of the twenty-first century cries out for the sort of leader who can take charge with quite a different approach. Do we have role models representing this type of leader, with whom we can be reflected? Do we have leaders who enjoy respect and understand how to act within a world context? Where do they come from, and what drives them? What do they see as their greatest assignment? How do they bring people together?

The type of leader required in the twenty-first century

The twenty-first century is an interesting but particularly complex era. There is a growing realisation that another type of leader is necessary to steer us through all the crises of the west – environmental problems, rising terrorism, the growing divide between rich and poor, the lack of trust between citizens and consumers, and the increasing awareness that things must change. We need leaders to build a tribal community, and whose most important objective is the well-being of the community rather than their own personal success. This demands special leaders.

The twenty-first century demands leaders in the luxurious position of possessing a balance where vision, courage, passion and compassion are united. This is the type of leader with a commanding personality, driven by a mission greater than himself, with inner resources, dreams and passion. He will be able to share and connect, and possess a sense of justice. He will not be a leader who limits himself to company practices. This form of leadership is not based on power, riches, public rights or favoured privileges. There is no question of telling tales against others or misusing power. These leaders do not become rich at the expense of others, nor do they allow corruption or extreme wealth to cause harm to their leadership.

These leaders think and work with great vision, promote connection and are generous. They are experts in their field, builders, peacemakers and champions of equality. This type of leadership unites social, physical, mental and spiritual dimensions. These leaders can motivate communities to cope with the themes and dilemmas which we stand for. These are leaders with humanity.

The Elders

The Elders, founded in 2007, is such a group of leaders. Assembled by Nelson Mandela and through the initiative of Richard Branson (Virgin) and Peter Gabriel (pop icon), they are a group of independent world leaders who use their influence together for world peace, the fight against human suffering and poverty, and to achieve equality for everyone, man and woman, young and old, black and white. The idea behind The Elders is the realisation that a new form of leadership is necessary in this strongly globalised world, using the analogy of the elderly members who originally fulfilled this role

'A leader . . . is like a shepherd. He stays behind the flock, letting the most nimble go out ahead, whereupon the others follow, not realising that all along they are being directed from behind.'

Nelson Mandela, *Long Walk to Freedom*, 1995

within tribal communities. The Elders consists of twelve members, amongst others Desmond Tutu, Jimmy Carter, Kofi Annan and Graça Machel (Nelson Mandela's current wife). They freely give independent advice to modern world leaders on solving global problems, and turning attention to common interests of people all over the world.

Among The Elders are a remarkable number of Nobel Peace Prize winners. This integrated and people-oriented form of leadership enjoys recognition and respect throughout the world. The Dutch Princess Mabel of Orange-Wisse Smit was General Director of the Elders for four years.

Great leaders and their followers?

Recent times have seen the rise of many great, wise leaders from the African continent, such as Govan Mbeki and Nelson Mandela, both from South Africa and founders of the ANC, Ellen Johnson Sirleaf from Liberia, the first woman president of Africa, and Barak Obama, first black president of the USA, with Kenyan roots. Another example is Kofi Annan, from Ghana, top diplomat, successful reformer, stimulator and bridge builder. We can also include Paul Kagame from Rwanda, who has recently been acclaimed by *Time* magazine as one of the hundred most influential leaders of the moment.

These leaders have all been celebrated for their knowledge, vision, skills, ability to connect and their decisiveness.

One example of a leader who knew how to win worldwide respect through his integrated and humanitarian form of leadership was Julius Nyerere, Tanzania's first elected president after independence in 1962. President Thabo Mbeki of South Africa said the following about Julius Nyerere's leadership:

'Love for the people and loyalty to their cause; commitment to the cause of peace; attachment to principle; honesty, humility and personal integrity; courage and a great intellect; the capacity to sustain hope at the most difficult moments; the determination to ensure that the sun shone over Africa, to banish the dark centuries which have been our heritage.'

Nyerere's nickname was *Baba wa Taifa*, or *Father of the Nation*, as Tanzania saw him. He was a modest man, calling himself a schoolmaster who had accidentally become president. His greatest ambition was to make his country a modern nation after the end of colonialism. In order to achieve this, he developed his own programme, based on self-motivation and self-reliance. Nyerere called this concept *Ujamaa* (the large family), comparable to a socialist government of self-supporting communities. He united Tanzania with Tanganyika and Zanzibar, and provided free education which put an end to widespread illiteracy. Hundreds of native Tanzanians were once again able to live and work together under his inspiring leadership. With his gently persuasive judgment, he was seen both far and wide as one of the greatest authoritative African leaders, and he resolved many conflicts on the African continent.

Dr. Wafula Okumu (Institute of Security Studies, Pretoria) spoke about leaders like Nyerere:

'African leaders have traditionally understood from the cradle that they had a moral, political and economic responsibility to serve their people in an ethical, trustworthy and transparent manner.'

Nelson Rolihlahla Mandela was the son of a local chieftain. He later became a lawyer by profession. Mandela's moving life story is known throughout the world, and has inspired many people, both young and old. He is universally praised for his fight against Apartheid and the way in which he lead his country to freedom. He achieved this by applying the norms and values he had acquired from his tribal background.

Realising dreams and ambitions

What these leaders all have in common is that none of them was content with the situation in which they and the people found themselves. They did not lose hope, but were strongly driven towards actions and developments which would improve their situation. This longing for improvement motivates creativity. Strong leaders do not live for personal fortune, rather for the pleasure of accomplishing their mission. Nelson Mandela was not concerned with personal gain or recognition, only equal rights for black and white.

In his book *'The Spiral of Creation'*, Marinus Knoope describes the stages from dream to reality. One of these stages is going against the flow, which you must resist: *'Mandela did not become an example for the nation by having the good fortune to be imprisoned. He became a role model through his ambition to change things.'* Mandela moved mountains with his positive vision, creativity and persistence.

Charisma and authenticity

Charisma, authenticity and leadership are strongly linked. Ernestine Gordijn, Professor of Social Psychology at Groningen's state university, defined charismatic people as having an obvious vision which they can clearly articulate. Their language is moving; they make frequent eye contact, and create strong links through body language. They can create the 'we-feeling'. They are often physically attractive, with a fresh, self-assured gaze, and are generally well-dressed.

Strong leaders are on a mission. They reach people in their own surroundings and place them on higher planes by their own authenticity. Through their own balance and ambitious sense of purpose, they can lead people around them, and challenge them to growth and significance.

'We are not loved because we are good, we are good because we are loved.'
Desmond Tutu

Stone Soup

Once upon a time, a soldier was making his lengthy way home after a war.

He was on foot, because he had no horse and the stagecoach was too expensive. He didn't have a penny. Dawn was breaking when, tired and hungry, he reached a little village.

The village dwellers had seen him coming from afar, and they stood looking at him suspiciously, as he took his kit bag from his back. He stretched and smiled.

A villager stepped up to him. He was worried, as he thought the soldier wanted food and drink. But the people were also hungry. The war had also come to the village, the harvest was plundered, and they had to share what was left.

Still the soldier smiled.

No, he needed no food, but if someone had a pan of water?

The farmer remembered that he had an old pot which he used for pig-feed.

The soldier could use it, as the pig had gone, and the village pump was in the square.

The soldier cleaned the pot thoroughly, filled it with water and set it on a fire of kindling wood.

When the water was boiling, he took a spoon and a shiny grey stone from his kit bag, and put the stone in the water. The villagers watched open-mouthed as the soldier told them he was making stone soup.

This stone would make the finest soup that had ever been eaten.

He tasted the pot's contents with the spoon, and nodded appreciatively. If he only had more salt, the soup would be even more delicious. Eventually somebody shuffled forward with a pinch of salt.

The soldier added it to the pot, and tasted the soup again: delicious! But a few bones would make it even better. Again, somebody appeared from the group with a few bones meant for the dog.

While he was tasting the soup again, the soldier said that a few potatoes would make it more nourishing, and yet again, someone approached him, this time with a small bowl of potatoes.

With a smile on his face, the soldier said how delicious the soup was, but that with some vegetables . . . now the village women came from all sides, one with an onion, another with two leeks, a cabbage, some carrots.

A wonderful smell was coming from the pot, when a farmer proudly came up to the soldier with a piece of bacon and a sausage. He had been keeping them for himself, but they would be even better in the soup.

That evening, the whole village ate the magnificent stone soup, and they all went to bed with full stomachs.

The next morning, when the soldier was ready to move on, the villagers asked if they could keep the miracle stone. Then they would never be hungry again.

The soldier gave them the stone, thanked them for their hospitality, and pressed them to make the soup exactly as he had done.

He swung his kit bag onto his back again and walked out of the village to his next destination.

Once out of sight, he bent down and picked up a round, grey stone, which he put in his bag, and humming, he went on his way.

Anonymous

It is vision, spirit and charisma which effects change in the behaviour of people, who can then accomplish their mission together with the leader. This is about the leaders, not their ego. They see success as something which can be jointly established. The satisfaction they experience from success comes from a collective result, not individual performance.

Creating a work place with spirit

A group can only be successful if there is a leader present who can boost and facilitate the group-process. Seth Godin, marketing expert and author of the management book *Tribes*, says this about leadership:

'Leaders are not 'führers', but people who take responsibility passionately, and use their talent and creativity to promote group-process'

Godin is not thinking about traditional managers here, because they are usually concerned with handling existing processes.

You would be fortunate, as a leader, to be born in a country with a story telling heritage, such as the African continent. Story telling is a special way to convey important events, appealing to the imagination. The twenty-first century needs good, inspiring stories, from personal experiences as well as from organisations. They can be about situations or people's actions, conduct and reorganisation. They can be told from the teller's perspective, in order to illustrate a meaning. If stories are based on one's own, deep experiences, they become a powerful mechanism for connecting people. Recognition and authenticity play a great role here, ensuring that people in their turn form connections with the story. A good story is characterised by a breakthrough, or an unexpected twist. There are moments of frustration, care or challenge, which the listener can recognise or imagine.

A story contains a message, a wise lesson or a moral. It can show an approach and a result. It can be told repeatedly to those who are open to it, and can form an important cornerstone of a community, movement or organisation. There is no sense in telling a story with no resonance. Behaviour and stories must be recognisably linear, or they are counter-productive.

'Just a few months ago we heard a whole story about People First. We were at the head of the organisation. Well, I don't know where we are now, after restructuring' **Multinational employee during reorganisation.**

It is often difficult for western leaders to be enthusiastic about their work places, even if they want to be. Performance training, well planned and designed Powerpoints, flashy techniques are only facilitated with the leader's authenticity, passion and story. This is exactly what gives leaders the chance to create a powerful community.

Creating value rather than profit

Strong leaders know about connecting the people around them. They therefore ensure that everyone realises the importance of strengthening themselves and their surroundings. It quickly becomes a matter of giving and receiving trust, understanding and transparency, for which leaders are the role models, leading by example. This gets the best out of their surroundings. They build a tribal community, which forms the basis of a very successful team. Due to personal experience, this team is better placed to look at clients' questions and concerns. Only when the team understands that it is not just about creating profit, is it time to look at creating value for the client.

This different way of thinking can only be accessible to a team, if it is also available for the organisation. Companies must make a profit, of course, but other values are important in the twenty-first century. The economic laws at the heart of the traditional western world are under severe pressure. Now it will be more about consideration of value instead of profit, which will provide the basis for team development and *community building*.

Martijn Aslander is the founder of Elvenstone, a particular network of remarkable people who are willing to share their knowledge, insight and contacts in an innovative manner (http:/elvenstone.com) He speaks about the consideration of value:

'I believe that our world can learn a great deal from complementary economies, which work with social and information capital above monetary capital. The fact is that the lion's share of our working methods relies on manual labour. My suggestion is to substitute thinking about profit with thinking about value. Our economy is still based on the struggle for profit maximalisation, which seldom leads to maximum profit. Companies are trying to reduce costs, by laying people off in times of crisis, for example, by reorganizing and to achieve more turnover in markets where they are active. In the near future, the fight for zero optimalisation – where I can be of most value – will be substituted for profit maximalisation. The Internet will make it possible for us to put our value in exactly the right place more quickly and easily than ever.''

Artikel Renson van Tilborg in *GITP Connect*

'A true master is not the one with the most students, but the one who creates the most masters.
A true leader is not the one with the most followers, but the one who creates the most leaders.
A true king is not the one with the most subjects, but the one who leads the most to kingship.
A true leader is not the one who knows the most, but the one who sees that others acquire the most knowledge'

Neale Donald Walsch, *Happier than God,* **2008**

Assignment for leaders in *the global arena*

Bringing energy, creativity and soul into their surroundings is the greatest assignment for leaders in these turbulent times, so that they can confront today's challenges. This is now of concern to their families, society, a team or an organisation.

Furthermore, it is the leader's task to create, facilitate, lead others and to inspire. A leader's own behaviour is the most important instrument. Good leadership in the twentieth century is impossible without a good balance between attitude, competencies and emotions. This balance gives them a sense of purpose and a desire to make a contribution to the world. They place concerns for their surroundings above those of themselves.

Even when in prison, Nelson Mandela knew about setting up and leading the powerful ANC with his authenticity and his tribal approach. He knew how to lead the country on the basis of the same philosophy. As one of the first enlightened spirits of his time, he demonstrated that tribal leadership is not only applicable to leading a community, but also an organisation or a country.

Concluding remarks

A new type of leader will come to the fore in the twenty-first century, who can teach the new world a great deal. It is of course interesting to determine exactly how Africa has produced many great leaders.

We know from African children that their upbringing within the community fosters strong values such as compassion, unselfishness and consideration. Mutual dependence, tendency to consensus and discussion belong to the old tribal values in African culture. They ensure that a community knew how to survive. These values are reflected in the ancient humanist philosophy of Ubuntu. This philosophy is widespread in various forms all over the Bantu countries of the African continent, and it is now more pertinent than ever. Its application in modern-day Africa has lead to a powerful, authentic African democracy. It has not been imposed by the west, but it is fed and sustained from within. Ubuntu can offer the West a means to overcome the great challenges of the twenty-first century.

It is time to have a look at this philosophy.

Ubuntu - a Lifeline

'Africans have a thing called UBUNTU; it is about the essence of being human, it is part of the gift that Africa is going to give the world. It embraces hospitality, caring about others, being willing to go that extra mile for the sake of another. We believe that a person is a person through other persons; that my humanity is caught up and bound up in yours. When I dehumanize you, I inexorably dehumanize myself. The solitary human being is a contradiction in terms, and therefore you seek to work for the common good because your humanity comes into its own in community, in belonging.'

Desmond Tutu, *The Right to Hope: Global Problems, Global Vision*, 1995

We are each born into a specific culture. This culture determines how we look at the world, and how the world in turn perceives us. We often only realise that we belong to one culture when we come into contact with another. Many world conflicts arise from the absence of respect and ignorance about another culture. We are making increasing contact with the norms and values of other cultures through globalisation, both individually and in our work. There is much that we can learn from this.

> *Where eastern cultures show us spirituality and western cultures show us technology, the southern cultures give us the opportunity to become acquainted with solidarity.*

Numerous tribes on the African continent are strongly dependent on solidarity for their well-being and survival of their community. They apply their familiar norms and values to all facets of their lives, which results in a deep feeling of security, respect and recognition. Nelson Mandela knew how to connect his very diverse fellow countrymen, separated by Apartheid, by making the most of their strongly-rooted feeling of solidarity. He gave the name 'Rainbow Nation' to his South Africa.
Africa can undoubtedly profit from western knowledge, technology and skills. But it can also offer something very special - a humanistic philosophy which can help the western world find significant answers to contemporary questions: the philosophy of Ubuntu.

The ethics of humanistic Ubuntu

Ubuntu (pronounced 'oo-BOON-too') or 'umuntu ngumuntu ngabuntu' is of Zulu origin, and means simply that a person is a person because of other people.
It is a common term in the African Bantu languages, and is seen as typically African. Many African people make use of Ubuntu in their own way, according to their own language, circumstances and beliefs.
In Botswana, for example, Ubuntu philosophy is known as 'Botho'. This philosophy is widespread, not only within the essence of the people, but also at governmental level. Botho is one of the five national principles in the *'Vision Statement: Driving Botswana to 2016'* after democracy, development, self-reliance and unity.
It is known as 'Umundu' in Kenya and 'Ubupfura' in Rwanda.

> *In 2008, Madonna wrote and produced a documentary about Malawi orphans, called 'I am because we are', a direct reference to Ubuntu, or 'uMunthu', as it is known in Malawi.*

Many African countries have their own word for this philosophy, but what is it really about? In conversation with Africans living with the Ubuntu principle, it is clear they find it hard to express. When asked, 'What does Ubuntu mean for you?', the answer seems almost blessed: 'That is what we are. Together. We belong to each other. This makes us happy. We are joined together.'

The reaction of these Africans shows how deeply anchored Ubuntu is in their humanity. The philosophy pivots, as it were, on social relationships mutually between people, and gives guidance to the manner in which these personal relationships are conducted. Therefore Ubuntu clearly shows that we cannot function without being part of a stronger connection.

Furthermore, we only learn to know ourselves by belonging to a group or community. It is precisely through such meetings with others that we can develop and grow. We can only succeed if the community to which we belong is successful. The function and survival of the group is more important than the success of the individual. This asks people to stop being so concerned with themselves. However it does not necessarily mean that the individual is unimportant, rather that the talent, the role and the value of every individual is recognised and used within the framework of the group interest.

Ubuntu touches one's whole life and being. It is the source of existence, a fundamental right, an expression of equality, common objectives and a shared destiny. It is anchored in African genes. Ubuntu is a way of life.

During the last few decades, we in the west have become distant from our surroundings and ourselves. We no longer feel so linked to our history. The rights of the individual have become more important than our connection with each other. Many people are now alone or egoistical. With all its big issues, this new time demands solidarity. The call for change will herald the call for solidarity. It is interesting to note how Ubuntu can achieve and foster this.

Stories, rituals, power and solidarity

Story telling has an important function in African tribal culture. Stories can revive history. Culture can be defined and developed in this manner. Stories can be about clarifying and managing relevant contemporary events and issues, gaining energy and hope or taking charge of difficult situations.

Real poverty

'Let me just tell you a story about real poverty. A very enthusiastic and concerned aid worker was sent to a village in a rural area by his organisation, with the instruction: 'Go and help fight poverty'.

The aid worker arrived at the appointed village, looked at the surroundings, at the dust in the square. He said to the people, 'I am searching for the greatest poverty, can you show me the way?' 'Well,' said the villagers, looking at each other and shaking their heads. 'Not here, in the square. There is no real poverty here, but perhaps in the narrow back streets.' And they took him there.

He saw a little hut in the back street, and entered through the curtain that served as a door. He was welcomed and began to speak. 'I understand that things are not easy for you. Are you suffering from poverty? I really want to help you.' 'Oh no, not here,' answered the people, surprised at the question. 'Perhaps the mayor can help you.' The aid worker got up, left the hut and went to the mayor. He said, ' I have come here to help with the fight against poverty. But I don't think people understand me. Can you tell me where the greatest need is? Because I want to make a start.' The mayor was completely taken aback, but he laughed and said 'My dear fellow, there is no poverty here, look around you. Can you see any poverty? Don't we have each other?'

Graça Machel, international advocate for women's and children's rights; former freedom fighter and first Education Minister of Mozambique, and married to Nelson Mandela, at an investment conference in Wassenaar, The Netherlands (2011)

A story like this offers people the opportunity to compare their world image with a different one. Stories are passed down through the generations in African culture, which ensures that cultural identity is retained. Stories help people from tribal cultures to know about the history of their ancestors, and to be connected to it.

In his book *African Tribal Leadership voor managers* (2007) Willem H.J. de Liefde states that story-telling is the foundation of culture:

'They form the reservoir of collective knowledge, and are the mechanism which shares and complements cultural heritage. Shared stories form bonds and create trust.'

There are more cultural rituals and cornerstones which tribal members enjoy and celebrate. Singing and dancing together help them make strong decisions. They sing about what they arrange in their lives, the extended family and solidarity with each other. It does not matter whether your role is that of leader, young or old, man or woman. Their communal singing and dancing is a joyful expression which strengthens their resolve, and enhances their experience of connectedness and positive energy.

Up-bringing, status and lineage

People in the west are given a certain status according to financial wealth, material well-being and career. They are enthusiastic followers of the philosophy of René Descartes – 'I think, therefore I am'. The individual and his development are central in every western cooperative, such as up-bringing, education, healthcare and enterprise, which are shaped by this individualistic perspective.

Issues such as age, gender, bloodlines and social relationships are more important in the African culture, with the family playing a pivotal role. This results in a child having an extended family of fathers, mothers, grandparents, uncles and aunts. Consequently, it is more than simply learning knowledge and skills; it includes behaviour, conduct and the importance of the group. Family solidarity is handed down to children during their up-bringing. Each story they hear resonates with kinship. Ancestral and community roots play a large role in African up-bringing.
Even unborn children are included in this kinship, so tribal cultures are very spiritually aware.

'It takes a village to raise a child.'
African proverb

'Rhythm is the architecture of being, the inner dynamic that gives it form, the pure expression of the life force. Rhythm is the vibratory shock, the force which, through our sense, grips us at the root of our being. (...) By doing this, rhythm turns all these concrete things towards the light of the spirit. In the degree to which rhythm is sensuously embodied, it illuminates the spirit.'
Léopold Senghor, poet, writer, and first democratically elected president of Senegal.

Africa knows their ancestors' stories and lessons in life very well. People in Coptic-Christian Ethiopia tell stories from their bloodlines, dating back to the biblical times of King David. Every Ethiopian knows the story of the Ark of the Covenant, which they believe rests in Aksum. Their energy, power and dignity are derived from these stories.

The solidarity which Ubuntu offers is a circular process. People fulfill an important and valuable role in the community, like links in a chain. They feel connected to both their ancestors and their unborn children. The norms and values of Ubuntu philosophy are passed down through the generations.

Leadership and the elderly

Within the broad context of family groups, we can see the most visible form of effective and connective leadership in Africa. An important role has been carved out for the community leader in tribal cultures, the Kgosi. This leader enjoys the trust and respect of everybody, and in fact is in service to them. Tradition determines his ambitions and agenda, while his knowledge and wisdom serve the community. He maintains good relations with other groups, and is open to outside developments that can have a healthy influence on his own. These relationships can be very important to the survival of the community. You are not simply accepted as a leader. Your position, gender, age, lineage and merits play an important role. Leadership is granted to you, and you must continually earn the privilege.

The elderly also have a large part in tribal cultures. Africans associate great age with wisdom and experience, which can be crucially important for the direction and survival of the group. The elderly have seen it all before, which makes them valuable advisors. Their wealth of experience is used to make choices and decisions. They are assigned to conflict resolution and restoring troubled relationships. Their knowledge and experience benefit everyone, sometimes actively within the arms of the whole community, but also sitting on benches in town parks, ready to give advice or mediation.

'There had been tensions and misunderstandings in my partner's family. I decided to go to the elders in the park to discuss what we should do. I felt relieved and light-hearted again. One of them offered to come with me to help clear the air.' **An African calls on the elderly in his community.**

The elderly remain respected and loved members of their communities all their lives. Care-homes for the elderly, as in the west, where they live isolated from their families, are unknown among tribal communities. The same goes for orphanages.

'Ah, the Dutch, a very interesting culture to develop.' **Comment made by Ato Megabiaw Tassew Gedamu, former mayor of Gondar, Ethiopia, in conversation about how the west deals with the elderly.**

Well-meaning western organisations and initiatives have built care-homes and orphanages in Africa over the last few years. But these western solutions to problems are not always suitable in an African context.

> '*I have lived in Europe for years, and I'm doing very well. Last year I went back to my village for the first time in years. I took a washing machine with me, to help my old grandmother's heavy workload. To my surprise, she was cross with me. She thanked me very much, but did not want it, despite my arguments. When I came back to my village a few weeks later, I understood why. My well-meaning actions robbed her of her tasks within the family, and therefore also her valuable position.*'
> **African woman returning to her roots.**

Fortunately, the west is beginning to realise that you must look for African solutions to African problems. Fewer aid organisations are building care-homes and orphanages, and are now setting up local projects instead.

Mutual solidarity and responsibility are therefore central to tribal cultures. This is interpreted by the decision circle LekGotla.

LekGotla

The chairman calls the LekGotla together whenever it is needed. It is the beating heart of the community, whose members discuss important issues. It is a highly democratic process where everyone takes part. Respect and attentiveness are hugely important during these consultations. LekGotla participants are consulted as people, not just because of their expertise, which means more insight around the table. Their broadly based dialogues mean that they can grow together, as it were, towards widely supported decisions.

After the chairman has listened to various people, they enter into a period of reflection and contemplation. Somebody might take an issue back to his grass roots for further consultation. Therefore, a LekGotla might consist of several gatherings, before the chairman can finally reach a conclusion. But as soon as it is over, the whole community publicly supports the decision. This makes a tribal community a stable group and a strong economic unity.

Family culture in motion

Meanwhile, tribal communities have become acquainted with western norms and values. Thanks to various technological developments, the western world has become within arm's reach. It follows that Africa wants to put poverty behind it, establish good education and effective healthcare. It is also very important to understand that they want to professionalise and broaden the enterprise that exists in the genes of their family culture.

'I have brought you all together to discuss an important issue for us all. I have asked you (A)

because of the great knowledge, experience and respect that you enjoy with the organisation

concerned. I have invited you (B) as our senior, because in your life you have frequently met a

comparable complex situation. I have invited you (C) because you have newly returned to us. In

the last few years you have studied far from our borders and seen the world. I have invited you

(D) as representatives of women who live and work in the area in question.'

Invitation from an Ethiopian mayor to his advisors to participate in a tribal gathering,

where the first foreign investor, GreenDreamCompany was present.

At the same time, family values which ensure solidarity are important to take into the twenty-first century. It would be prudent to make use of western knowledge and technology, and if necessary to critically examine and determine individual values. These values go hand-in-hand with a process of decline and fall, as has been shown by the current crises. The challenge for African tribal culture is to preserve their familiar structure in the twenty-first century. These structures can form the basis for more social and economic prosperity. The way forward for these tribes is strongly dependent on how their leadership further develops.

Concluding remarks

Ubuntu allows an individual to put his relationships with others into order on various levels. It is interesting to note how the ancient humanist philosophy still seems to be enormously valuable and fundamental to the structure of the newly emerging Africa of the twenty-first century.

Ubuntu in Contemporary Africa

4

'Neither flying or walking on water are miracles.
No – the miracle is in walking on this earth, in this reality daily.'

**Liepollo l. Pheko, director of Trade Collective,
South Africa**

Ubuntu in its purest form belongs to pre-colonial Africa. Africa has taken things into its own hands since the abolition of Apartheid and the end of traditional colonialism. The continent itself is on a voyage of discovery, and is taking its place on the world's stage. It is successfully achieving this through its own democratic system, which is trying to preserve its authenticity on one hand, while at the same time making connections with the norms and values of modern times. Meanwhile, six out of ten growth economies are emerging from the African continent. This ensures the rise of a firmly broad-based middle class. Western powers have certainly influenced this development, but Nelson Mandela, as the first African leader, showed that tribal norms and values are both applicable and accessible at the highest level of society.

How can the authentic tribal values which are anchored to Ubuntu philosophy be implemented in, for example, modern politics, jurisdiction, education, healthcare, government and the role of women? Is there any relevance with the west?

Ubuntu in politics and jurisdiction

Within the politics of contemporary Africa, the importance of the elite or winning a debate is irrelevant. The Ubuntu concept is used to stress that there must be consensus in a political decision. This means that the relationship between government and people must be trust-based.

Botswana is a country that has integrated and formalised Ubuntu philosophy within its political structure most successfully. It is a densely populated country, admittedly with a government, but also with a crucial role given to tribal leaders. They give advice about complex issues which Parliament might not be able to solve or wish to approach. These tribal leaders take the issue right back to grass-roots level for discussion and decision-making. Then they can give answers to Parliament with the advice of their community. This approach generates popular support, which contributes to the country's stability. Botswana has meanwhile developed into a country with an extremely investment-friendly climate.

Ubuntu is also applicable in contemporary African jurisprudence, certainly in a specific way, with humanity at the centre. From a strongly human perspective, legal administration seeks solutions to problems in ensuring humanity for both perpetrators and victims. In this way, African jurisprudence assumes shame instead of guilt, truth instead of cunning, forgiveness instead of revenge, mediation and reconciliation instead of confrontation and accountability.

This is an acceptable way of reaching reciprocal and acceptable standards of solutions to strained and broken relationships between individuals or communities. A value-based recovery of harmony in a relationship is therefore more important than estrangement, retribution or arguments about who is right. Ubuntu aims to achieve a change in conduct, and realises that community resocialisation is more important than a penalty system.

'As I walked out the door toward the gate that would lead to my freedom, I knew if I didn't leave my bitterness and hatred behind, I'd still be in prison.'

Nelson Mandela

The Truth and Reconciliation Commission hearings took place in South Africa during the nineties. Perpetrators asked forgiveness of their victims, who gladly granted it. The objective was to restore truth and humanity to both perpetrator and victim alike. They would only then be free to continue their lives, through finding each other.

The Ubuntu Centre in Burundi, based on Ubuntu principles, focuses on the process of war trauma on individuals, families and communities. Its psychological training programmes successfully work towards the peace, reconciliation and restoration of this war-ravaged country. These programmes are aimed at both individuals and communities, who are both essential for psychological re-integration. The centre uses theatre and story telling to restore dialogue.

Another example is Rwanda, the land of a thousand hills. The whole world knows Rwanda because of the violence of the Hutu and Tutsi genocide. Twenty years later, the country is now more prosperous than ever. With President Paul Kagame at its helm, the country has become fully democratic, and one of Africa's strongest emerging economies. What is the secret of its success? Ubuntu, or at least the power of forgiveness. Hutu and Tutsi found each other again in their Rwandan identity, able to see each other clearly as human beings, working together for the development of their beautiful country.

Ubuntu in education

The concerns of a community, including education, are central to tribal culture. It is very important that someone contributes to his community via his studies. He will learn to support the survival of the community through his own means, and to guarantee the social system and process, together with the needs of the community.

'But anger, resentment, desire for revenge, greed, even aggressive competition which dominates our contemporary world affect and endanger our harmony. Ubuntu indicates that those who want to commit atrocities and inhumanities are themselves victims, of a general ethos, political ideology, an economic system, or a distorted religious conviction. As a result, they are just as dehumanised as those they seek to crush.'

Desmond Tutu

It is not uncommon for a community itself to allow someone from its midst to begin studies, who fully trusts that his acquired knowledge and insights can in turn benefit the community. African students studying in the west also talk about wanting to study in order to mean something for their family and community back home. This is exactly what the Macheta tribe from South Africa did, in letting someone from their community study law. Now, after Apartheid, the process of giving back is fully on target, and this lawyer promotes his community's concerns in order that the land of his forefathers can benefit.

A good illustration of how Ubuntu works in the education system is the CIDA City Campus (CIDA), founded in 2000 and established in Johannesburg, South Africa. The passionate focus of CIDA University is towards young under-privileged Africans, who would not normally have access to higher education. While the costs of higher education in South Africa have risen enormously recently, CIDA is able to offer business degrees to students without financial contributions from the Department of Education, but instead with the help of generous donors such as Oprah Winfrey. What is the secret of their success? The answer is both simple and complex: passion, solidarity and self-confidence.

CIDA has added modules to their curriculum which appeal to the students' community feeling. They learn to practise and apply these modules in their own community. Their example encourages young community members to begin studies in their turn. But what is perhaps most remarkable is that these students run the university together like a community as part of their study. They do everything with their teachers, from large-scale maintenance and cleaning, to managing the library. CIDA wants to educate and provide South Africa's new leaders along the way – professionals who know how to step aside, placing community concerns above their own.

This community-philosophy has even encouraged many former CIDA students to voluntarily give lessons, provide student support and generally to remain involved.

Mrs. Liepollo l. Pheko is a leading South African political analyst, teacher, social activist and director of Trade Collective. This is a think-tank engaged with political economy, international business, immigration, and good citizenship, which creates links between these and themes such as gender, ethnicity and society. She made a speech for new CIDA graduates in 2010 (see appendix) which showed how modern education is putting Ubuntu principles into practice. One passage from her farewell speech states:

'We do not always have to be the most clever or loudest or have the best singing voice in the room. And if by chance we are, it is advisable to invite smarter people or those with lovelier voices ... or find a different room. In professional circles it is called networking. In organisations it's called team building. And in life it is called family, friends, and community. We are all gifts to each other, and my own growth as a leader has shown me again and again that the most rewarding experiences come from my relationships. And it sure keeps me humble and keeps my singing voice in perspective.'

The individual and his performance are central to western culture. The pupil focuses so much on himself that this strongly globalised world is led into confusion. It is more important than ever to know how other cultures learn, think, feel and act in the twenty-first century. We must step out of our own shadow to connect with a larger whole. In this sense, the new world offers us great chances and possibilities for a better life.

Ubuntu in religion and spirituality

In tribal cultures, we see a strong bond between forefathers, spirits and children yet unborn, who all inhabit another world. Ancestral spirits from five generations earlier remain active in life through stories and rituals. Being a respected community member means earning such an honour, even after death.

This worship can lead to an extremely complicated, yet fascinating world of faith, such as in Madagascar. During the Famadihana, or interment, families remove all the dead from their hereditary vaults. They take them round, dancing and celebrating, to show the living the continued significance of the dead. This is a form of contact with spirituality. Ubuntu is also seen as a spiritual source, whose approach is reflected in healing rituals, restoring the balance between God and humans. The sick can only become healed through restored balance. Dirk J. Louw from the University of the North writes, *'This unity emerges from the idea that we are all parts or aspects of the same universal forcefield.'*

Africa does not know the linear time concept which the western world has adopted. Ubuntu is a circular philosophy which assumes the circle of life. During colonialism, of course, missionaries had a huge influence on Africa's original religion and spirituality. In many cases, the imposition of Christianity and Islam has completed a process of suitability and acceptance, which incorporates typical African symbolism and rituals.

Ubuntu in institutionalism

People in modern-day Africa are busy integrating tribal cultural skills into institutional organisations so that a typical African variant of liberalisation and democracy can be achieved. Ubuntu also helps people to connect at this level. This means that South Africa knows how to transform itself from a country divided by Apartheid into a multi-cultured rainbow nation, not based on differences, but a gathering of mutual concerns among the community.

Around the turn of the century, it was Africa's ambition to develop its own identity after colonialism, and to tackle the poverty of the continent with an African approach. This lead to the establishment of the New Partnership for Africa's Development (NEPAD), a development plan founded by and for African leaders to radically address under-development and African marginalisation, with its own cultural identity as the basis, rather than following a western model. A large group of African leaders within NEPAD committed themselves, from the new African identity, to collaborating towards peace, democracy, security, knowledge development, and effective administration. In this way, NEPAD leaders oblige foreign companies to cooperate with their plan for African democracy and development. These companies in turn feel obliged to contribute to good leadership, for example, together with organisational development and society. Through accepting their social responsibilities, they support today's Africa in achieving their ambitions. More than two hundred companies doing business in Africa have committed themselves to NEPAD's guidelines. NEPAD has therefore become a platform of opportunity, which provides an African solution to the fight against poverty.

Ubuntu and healthcare

Because Ubuntu is intertwined with the daily life and well-being, Africa has developed traditional healthcare which serves every community. Standards, taboos, traditions and culture form the pillars of this traditional medicine, which has been able to survive years of colonialism, and passed on from generation to generation. Africa certainly makes use of regular medical healthcare, but it is chronic patients in particular who have eventually found their way back to traditional healthcare, with all its attention to traditions and communities, and its intimate knowledge of the patient, for whom traditional medicine is often their last hope.

The value of traditional medicine and its practitioners is gaining increasing respect from regular medicine. In many countries, this has lead to a collaborative policy and

'South Africans had a heritage that helped them face more than challenges, and a value system that guided their behaviour at the individual, family and community level. We have a responsibility to use the positive attributes of Ubuntu to build a nonracial, nonsexist and united South Africa. There is no dispute that we are a diverse society. All of us have consistently urged that we use this diversity as a strength to unite our people. But within the diversity, are dominant values that bind communities together and ensure social cohesion. These values drive communities to act in solidarity with the weak and the poor, and help community members behave in a particular way for the common good.'

President Mbeki (2005), www.dfa.gov.za

regulations framework, which has increased knowledge and skills. Traditional medical knowledge is therefore protected, and modern healthcare realises more about the use of living resources, and the two become integrated. African countries can scale up local products by knowing more about the medicines used in traditional methods, which will lead to improved medication.

The African continent is still facing the problem of HIV and Aids. The impact of these epidemics is enormous, and every level of society is affected. They infect and destroy the lives of individuals and communities, and can cripple entire economies. This has far-reaching consequences for the social, political and economic environment. Culture plays a large role in introducing the need to practise safe sex, as the social system and traditions within communities mean that approaching this subject can be difficult and sensitive.

These epidemics have been the subject of much global attention in recent decades. Methods have been developed across the world to tackle the problem. The most successful programmes connect with the culture of the communities. They make full use of consultative structures, storytelling to convey the most effective practices, and singing and dancing during campaigns and training. Afterwards, community members can follow cultural transformation training, in an attempt to bring suitable infrastructure improvements into being.

Ubuntu and gender
Women play a great social and connective role in communities, yet they are still not very prominent in

history. There are many strong African female role models, but they are not always presented as such. Professor Musa Dube from the University if Botswana would like to bring about change. She makes a plea for awareness via storytelling:

'Storytelling which is central to African life, should be used by women as a theory of analysis and as a method of rewriting the patriarchal silences about women's lives in the biblical texts and African history. This is a very important discovery because this provides essential contextual analytical frameworks.'

In fact, she is pleading for a tribal mechanism to effect change, and so improve the role and self-confidence of women.

Next to healthcare projects, many business programmes are designed for women in Africa. The impact of support for these women is enormous, because the effects are immediately felt within their communities. African women are also very supportive of each other. Education and business programmes make full use of IT and Skype in their training methods:

Female entrepreneurship course member
Meanwhile, it is becoming increasingly clear that African women make outstanding professionals and effective entrepreneurs. They are becoming better represented on the jobs market, and feel connected with other women. It often seems that they choose to make use of other women's talents, and they pursue their own activities with a view to being of service to each other. IT knowledge plays a great role in this. It offers women

a broader palette of possibility such as education, employment and entrepreneurship. The African female professional, manager and businesswoman is now here to stay.

'I never knew I could be taught to use the computer online without physical contact by the trainer. I had always seen myself as a novice and could not have learned anything IT. But after spending the weekly period in the Skype meetings with the authors' gentle guidance, I have discovered remarkable things about myself. I have grown more to accept myself and developed great faith in myself.'

Ubuntu as the basis for sustainable economic growth and development
In an economic sense, Africa is flourishing. It is not experiencing the same economic crisis as we are in the west. The continent is rapidly catching up. What is happening to the tribal norms and values in these growth economies?

Tanzania is a good example of a country making a large economic growth breakthrough, and understanding how to make use of Ubuntu. After independence from England in 1961, President Nyerere launched a programme of economic recovery and growth, based on the tribal community system. Nyerere called this programme Ujamaa, which is in fact one of the numerous African variations of Ubuntu. Nyerere translated his Ujamaa into a political-economic development model, whose democratic model wielded social, economic and political equality. He also nationalised several important economic sectors, and brought together a number of local products, which enabled mutual reinforcement. He increased Tanzanian self-confidence, where everyone provided a contribution, in an economic sense, as much to the group as individually. Above all, Tanzania learned to stand on its own two feet. Through Ujamaa, Nyerere made the translation into education: he established free compulsory education for every Tanzanian. He saw an opportunity to convey the principles of Ujamaa through education to Tanzanians. He appointed Swahili after English as the national official language, to reinforce unity and independence, which meant the building of a strong Tanzanian identity. The country made huge strides under his leadership, not only in an economic sense, but also in the improving healthcare – child mortality was greatly reduced, and life expectancy increased. Education became available to men and women alike. Illiteracy among the elderly was reduced by 75%.

Ujamaa was dismissed in the west for a long time as a primitive approach. However, it proved a solid basis for contemporary Tanzania. With the principles of Ujamaa as a basis, Julius Nyerere ensured significant economic and political change with his leadership and steadfastness, which won him world respect. The country enjoyed an annual economic growth rate of between 5 to 8.5%, thanks to a democracy based on tribal values.

Nyerere's typical African approach and results inspired many other leaders on the African continent to follow suit. Consider Ghana, South Africa, Botswana, and indeed Liberia, which is now experiencing strong growth under its first female president, Ellen Johnson-Sirleaf.

African Renaissance

After a long period of colonial looting and degradation, peace and stability on the continent are now more important than ever. A wind of hope and optimism blew over the continent after the release of Nelson Mandela in 1990, and the resulting process of democracy in South Africa. It has developed its own democratic model, where education, supported by the opportunities of IT and e-schools make it possible for people to work towards a lasting future. There now exists solidarity on the African continent.

This has not gone unnoticed by the rest of the world. There are now many investment locations in Africa, not only for African but also foreign investors and multinationals. Community members have now spread worldwide, and despite settling well in a new fatherland, they still have strong roots in their country of origin. These children of two cultures are known as *diasporas*. They invest together more in their homeland than in the work development sector.

China and India have shifted their expansion focus from Europe and America to Africa. Now that oil has been discovered in Angola, Sudan and Guinea, Africa has suddenly become very desirable. Better still for the African continent is that the now stronger Angola has been able to help its former colonial power, Portugal, currently struggling economically, with investments. This is a fine example of Ubuntu. The old world does not exist anymore. It is a world upside-down.

The African continent is now asking how it can bring cultural traditions to the twenty-first century. Because Africa is developing its own response to social, political and economic areas, the answer, when it is found, will have lasting results. How should the post-colonial relationship with western and international society be shaped? How will the continent hitch itself to globalisation and integration? This enormous challenge was christened the *African Renaissance* by the South African President Thabo Mbeki in 1998. A definition of

'As we speak of an African Renaissance, we project into both, the past and the future. I speak here of the emergence of Homo Sapiens on the African continent, of African works of art in South Africa that are over a thousand years old. I speak of the continuum in the fine arts that encompasses the varied artistic creations of the Nubians and the Egyptians, the Benin bronzes of Nigeria and the intricate sculptures of the Makonde of Tanzania and Mozambique. I speak of the centuries-old contributions to the evolution of religious thought made by the Christians of Ethiopia and the Muslims of Nigeria. When I survey all this and much more besides, I find nothing to sustain the long-held dogma of African exceptionalism, according to which the colour black becomes a symbol of fear, evil and death.'

President of South Africa Thabo Mbeki (1998)

this term, adopted throughout the continent, appears on the following page.

Following the example of this vision, the South Africans are making successful use of the BEE programme (Black Economic Empowerment) to achieve more equality between black and white Africans. This programme has enabled black professionals to reach the work floor. Now, fifteen years later, the first black management in a company is a real fact. This represents a new generation of leaders, whose cultural values from their childhood have become integrated into their leadership style.

Concluding remarks
Great African leaders attribute the strongly ideological and binding character of Ubuntu as a basis for the

African Renaissance. Ubuntu is now able to take its rightful place on the world's stage, which means that the African Renaissance can serve as an example for the western world. Ubuntu in fact offers to the western world suggestions and requirements for a better life, both for the individual and his surroundings, and for sustainable economic development. This wealth of opportunities and chances are completely suited to the challenges faced by the western world in this century.

The Organisation
as a Community

'He who travels alone will be eaten by a lion'
African proverb

The African continent has successfully integrated tribal norms and values into society. In the previous chapter, we saw the role of Ubuntu in different sectors. Due to the emerging African economies and the admission of the black African in companies and organisations, a new cultural identity is rising from within. Managers who grew up with trusted tribal values are occupying increasingly more crucial positions within organisations. How does this translate to the workplace? How do African managers provide leadership? And how do employees participate in a tribal organisation? How can the western world apply these lessons in its own organisations?

Change from within rather than imposition

The impact of the western approach, culture, science, religion, technology and language has always been enormous, as well as widely accepted, both as an ide-alised image, and through inability to react against it. But change is on the way. Africans call it the African Renaissance, which is currently taking place due to strong movement from within. Africa is rediscovering its own possibilities, power and values, and is looking for every opportunity to interpret these well. Western knowledge, experience and investment, and increasingly from the East, are both desirable and welcome, but it has been clear for some time that simply imitating tried-and-tested western organisation and leadership models does not work. The African continent is making huge progress by respecting people's drive and concern on one hand, with their strong wish for independence and responsibil-ity on the other. Tribal norms and values have caused a sensation with the emergence of organisations and a new middle class. They are now automatically finding their own organic way into organisations and companies.

Companies will therefore function as communities, where their leaders show themselves to be both con-necting and serving. Fons Trompenaars, professor of cross-cultural management at the Free University, The Netherlands , shares this view:

'If it is true that the nurturant community is the cradle of individualism, then it follows that many changes could be made to organizations, shaping them as communities that could increase rather than decrease the individuality of each member.'
Fons Trompenaars and Charles Hampden-Turner,
Riding the Waves of Culture, 1993

Fundamental tribal values within organisations

Tribal organisations assume a different human and world image. They are recognisable by their mutual strong connections and kinship. Organisations function and are led in the same way as communities. Ubuntu's circular principles are clearly central in these organisations: respect, trust, courage, entrepreneurship, compassion and dignity.

Respect and trust

People want to interact respectfully with each other. An honest encounter can only happen when there is respect. Treating someone respectfully means that there is a genuine interest in what drives the other person, and that you want to engage on a deeper level with them to really understand and appreciate them. Then there is room to confront unfinished business together with dialogue which will lead to a peaceful and constructive solution. Respect is mutual. You will challenge others to behave respectfully if you conduct yourself in the same manner, and can focus on finding solutions rather than apportioning blame for the cause of a problem.

Trust is a gift for each other. Together with respect, it creates a positive climate within an organisation. If people trust one another, they rely on, and feel responsible for supporting each other and reaching a result together. If you are full of trust, and know that the people around you are respectful, you dare to voice your ideas and face challenges. The others realise that you have the best interests of the group at heart, and you reach results together. It is never an individual performance.

With trust in an organisation's leadership, employees assume that it is always on their side, making team issues always a priority, and supporting where possible.

Courage and entrepreneurship

Courage is also necessary to be able to make good decisions, and these can sometimes be difficult. A leader is ready to give the best answers and make wise choices through talking openly and searching for dialogue. Wrong decisions are not glossed over or ignored, but recognised and restored. Knowing that making mistakes is part of life ensures that people will dare to try anything.

You take courses for the benefit of your organisation, not for personal gain. Then a creative climate will exist, giving ideas the chance to develop. Because people realise that they are valued by the organisation, and can exercise influence, they come forward. They take responsibility for their development, the organisation's quality and reaching the intended result, because they have complete trust that others will do the same.

Enterprise is part of every position and level of the organi-

sation. People do not point to each other to bring out improvement, and they do not wait for everything to be arranged to perfection. They enjoy being challenged to make a contribution through their own efforts, so they can take into account the impact that a decision has on life and work environments. After all, the *'extended context' fits the philosophy 'I exist because of we'*

> *'People are invited to create their own society'*
> **Willem de Liefde,** *African Tribal Leadership voor managers,* **2007**

Compassion and dignity

If you approach people with humanity, they feel loved and valued, because you are taking their needs and passions into account. When they realise that they are striving to invest in reaching the intrinsic value of others, they ensure a great flowering of humanity. To achieve this, people should see others as dignified equals, regardless of their own role or position. In this context, dignity is what is seen in others. If people know that they are valued, and enjoy respect, they feel worthwhile. There is no thought of subordinates in the level structure of a tribal organisation, which means that a strong leader approaches his employees from a perspective of human value rather than superior attitude. If people feel truly connected with each other, there exists a dynamic of positive energy which can lead to great results. These

'I was so happy! It was finally here. We had acquired the location where we would realise our eco-resort – a wonderful location on Lake Tana in Ethiopia. The ground had been measured and the contract fixed. The next thing to do was the Environmental Impact Report. I was thinking about measuring every dust particle, and also the effect the building and its materials would have on Nature. Easy! But of course it was more than that. Much more had to be submitted. Research into the project's effect on the surrounding community had to be carried out. What would it mean for them? We had to consider the potential contribution of the project on the entire surrounding area, such as the possibilities for education and employment for the local population. How could the project contribute to their healthcare and gender equality? That is what it was about''

Léon van Rijckevorsel,

co-founder GreenDreamCompany

aspects are reciprocal in character, as they reinforce each other.

The power of diversity

People are different, not only in terms of age and gender, but also because of their personal qualities, predisposition and talent. They can be from various religious backgrounds or atheists. Tribal organisations identify and acknowledge diversity, whose power can teach people about each other. They assume, quite naturally that everyone is unique, and they value people for their talents and qualities, not simply for their professional use to the organisation.

The whole person as a starting point

The fact that a tribal organisation values every aspect of its employees, means that much more than their professional expertise can be used. Their other qualities and different roles that they fulfill in their lives can also be advantageous for the progress and development of the organisation or community.

In this way, an individual is valuable to the community, and vice-versa. Furthermore, the community's value is determined by the significance to the surroundings, other communities or companies. This value shows the extent to which the well-being of other communities can be promoted. Reciprocity is a matter of course.

Vital organisations

The big difference with western organisations is that tribal ones are driven by trust, soul and purpose, while those in the West are used to being driven by the product, the service and the value to the shareholders. They keep track of developments among the competition, and look carefully at gaps in the market.

Tribal organisations are level, and based on a long tradition of solidarity. Achieving objectives together is central to them. There is not a top-down, bottom-up approach. People share their problems and dilemmas, and celebrate their successes together. A result is only successful when it is in harmony with its surroundings.

The IT company Axiz makes use of a tribal management model based on Ubuntu. 75% of its employees are black, and around 40% are women. Staff may also buy shares in the company.

'This means,' according to Bheki Sibeko, 'that since they became owners. their pride has returned.' Axiz experiences low levels of absenteeism, and there is practically no staff turnover. Axiz might resemble a social institution, but Sibeko stresses the business interest. 'We had great trouble with workers stealing the stock, but when the company came into the hands of the workers themselves in 2003, this loss declined by 80%. This is logical, because you don't steal from yourself, of course.' So African management is not only good for motivating the work force. 'We also make a lot of profit.'
From a publication by Mariëtte Heres,
www.Deondernemer.nl (2008)

You take responsibility together, regardless of your position. Being able to let go and delegate means trusting in others' qualities, and that truth plays a great role. Contact with others is central. There are no hidden agendas. If everyone dares to commit themselves, and feel valued as human beings, a positive and crucial

energy is set free, and they feel involved in their work. The resulting collective character makes these tribal organisations very strong, resilient and vital.

The tribal organisation leader

In organisations whose management is based on the tribal system, the leaders at the helm are strongly connected and closely linked to their employees. It is their job to turn their organisation into a flourishing community, to keep it together and to serve it. Tribal organisation leaders stand right at the heart. This is embodied by servitude, which is very different from western leaders, who tend to operate alone, and have to steer towards share value, which a company knows how to maximise for its shareholders. Tribal leaders know how to create a climate of trust, where people are encouraged to grow and learn from their mistakes. They are intuitive listeners, they know how to stimulate and motivate people and give them self-confidence. They are able to approach everything, including the company, from a wide context, which means that they put the *'I exist because of we'* principle into practice.

This is evident in the communication, decisions and choices of an organisation or society. A good leader must be flexible and willing to strive for a higher ideal. He must be able to give and share with others. His own ambitions and issues are inferior to those of the organisation.

'Before Apartheid, the Lebowa Platinum Mines in Limpopo, South Africa, had some white managers who were unfamiliar with the tribal culture of their employees. There was often tension and theft. After Apartheid, a black manager, who fulfilled his function based on familiar tribal principles, was recruited. He began by listening to the workers, and to consult them about decisions. He listened to their stories and dilemmas. He introduced familiar rituals into the company for them, such as singing, dancing and story telling. And he also ensured that the company invested in the communities where the people came from. Following on from all this, the management guru and great champion of tribal management Lovemore Mbigi was invited to work on linking the black and the white management. 'It was the first time that we all had lunch at one table together,' says Manyanga. And the whites even sang and danced with us later.' Initially, the white managers did not see much good in this, until they saw that the relationship with the surrounding communities and the employees rapidly improved, which was also visible in the company's results.'

From: *Paul Rosenmöller en ... de kracht van Afrika* (documentaire NCDO)

Decision-making through dialogue and truth sharing

The process of decision-making in tribal organisations is completely different from western ones. Tribal organisations make use of the traditional meeting-structure (LekGotla). Decisions are reached through joint dialogue and consultation with all concerned. The common issue is paramount, and they seek a collective solution.

Everyone is welcome to attend the meetings, all input is important. Somebody's actual function within an organisation is just one facet. Tribal meetings can transcend organisations. If external advice becomes necessary, to clarify the impact of a decision on the environment, for example, consultation will result. In this sense, Africa has worked for a long time with programme management.

The individual is more central in western organisations. This means that solutions are often more related to the issues of a small group or an individual. You may only take part in a meeting by invitation, and it is often the case that your function within the organisation is more important than your intrinsic qualities.

Participants in a tribal meeting communicate respectfully and attentively with each other. The leader throws open the matter to the group, and listens carefully to their reactions and opinions. Because everyone listens actively to each other, they grow, as it were, towards the best solution.

Truth is central in tribal organisations. Truth sharing in western organisations often leads to deadlock and a hardening of attitude. Background hidden agendas frequently play a part. An open dialogue leads to breathing space. People in tribal organisations have the courage to express themselves, because they always put the group's concerns above everything else.

Power, strong convictions and negotiating skills are very important in western organisations. Those who shout loudest get results. These may often be short-lived, however, as they are based more on individualism.

A tribal meeting can be constructed of various different sessions. It is not always the case that an agreement can be reached after the first meeting. They allow time for reflection and contemplation. After hearing everything during the meeting, the leader and participants adjourn to process new insights. The leader reaches a conclusion only when all issues are clearly in view. This decision will have maximum support, because everyone has been involved in the same growth process. Therefore the group concern soars above individual issues. Through this mutual solidarity, people feel part of the greater whole.

The cycle of decision, growth and direction

Culture is not static, but is always susceptible to change. This counts for both ethnic and organisational cultures. Tribal organisations always examine their position within the environment. Their very existence derives from their context, because they belong to a constantly changing environment, which is completely normal for them. They are open to change, because they realise that their context never stands still. They broach issues with an open mind, and apply the same cyclical approach as they do to their own lives. This process of diagnosis, examination and positioning occurs mostly during tribal meetings. The issues are illustrated with stories, metaphors and pictures. The decisions they reach in this manner are characterised by a durability which allows both drive and direction.

Western organisations make a SWOT analysis (Strengths, Weaknesses, Opportunities, Treats) to determine their positions and possibilities for growth and development. They experience an opportunity or a threat as things requiring action. Tribal organisations work from a position of respect for the context. If they feel threatened by, for example, another strongly emergent organisation, they decide together what it means for their own organisation and the people who work there. They can then define the right course of action.

Times recognises another dimension

Tribal organisations spend a lot of time on decision forming in order to provide enough support. Making a decision is too important not to allow sufficient time. Westerners find this difficult and inconvenient, because time is money, from their perspective. It can sometimes take a long time to reach a conclusion and decide on the next steps.

Concluding remarks

Western organisations are founded on the individual philosophy which advanced during the industrial revolution and the influence of colonialism. Conducting an open dialogue based on equality is not something recognised by an individualistic culture. At the same time, the West values entrepreneurship, education and healthcare, for example, together with the enormous amount of technical knowledge now available. The crisis has clearly demonstrated that many achievements can be fragile and short-lived, which results in dissatisfaction in the way people interact with each other, commerce, nature and the environment.

'The twenty-first century demands a new, modern system which does justice to human dignity, equality and solidarity, said Roemer in Amsterdam. Such a system consists of one thing – cooperation. It was Professor Ruud Galle, the expert in this field, who entered into the fray during a night-time radio broadcast with the idea that such solidarity is much more important than striving exclusively to make a profit. The cooperative approach does not lead to immediate wealth, which has plunged us into disaster; it is rather a long-term strategy that sees the members' concerns, including future generations, as paramount. This offers perspective in hard times, especially as sustainability is part of cooperative philosophy.'
Alphons Huiskes, 2011, http://grotewoorden.tctubantia.nl

Collective Africa's tribal leadership style and organisational model is returning to the world's stage with a new energetic approach. They perceive the western individualistic idea as belonging to the time of Apartheid and colonialism. However, Africans are open to learning from this, as they gain in technical knowledge and opportunities. How can we combine the best of both worlds? What contributions can western and tribal organisations make?

Ubuntu Meets the West

'Kyk, ek bou vir my 'n land
Waar 'n vel niks tel nie,
Net jou verstand.
Waar geen bokgesig in 'n parlement
kan spook om dinge permanent
verkramp te hou nie.
Waar ek jou kan liefhê
langs jou in die gras kan lê
sonder om in 'n kerk 'ja' te sê.
Waar ons snags met kitare sing
en vir mekaar wit jasmyne bring.
Waar ek jou nie gif hoef te voer
as 'n vreemde duif in my hare koer.
Waar geen skeihof
my kinders se oë sal verdof.
Waar swart en wit hand aan hand
vrede en liefde kan bring
in my mooi land.'

'Look, I'm building a new country where skin means nothing, only your mind. Where no goat-faced parliament can ever haunt or cramp you. Where you and your love can lie in the grass without saying 'I do' in church. Where we sing to guitars at night and bring each other white jasmine. Where I do not need to pour poison on you, the strange dove cooing in my hair. Where no parting shall dim the eyes of my children. Where hand in hand, black and white can bring peace and love to my beautiful country.'

**Antjie Krog,
'Kroonstad High School Yearbook',
from : Om te kan asemhaal, 1999**

Despite very different departure points, the African continent and the western world want to be as one. They each value a future for themselves and their children, with a need for connection, authenticity, happiness, perception and ethics. In other words, we all want to live in a better world, focused on global, cosmopolitan cooperation.

The beauty of the transitional phase in which we now find ourselves, is that there is fortunately room for enrichment. A logical conclusion in this time of crisis could be that western leaders, organisations and companies incorporate tribal values, in order to deliver added value. Are there any successful examples in the western world to show that this could happen? And how can Africa learn and take advantage of what the West has to offer? These two worlds can then meet each other frankly with equal needs and concerns. Is it possible for these two worlds to make use of a broader tribal understanding and enterprise requirements, in order to enlarge, reinforce and make more sustainable the quality of international cooperation and business?

A new point on the horizon

The individualistic era is now in decline. It does not seem to be the logical answer to big issues now or in the near future. Furthermore, if the West persists in this individualistic direction, it will fall behind on the world's stage. Meanwhile, the call for more cooperation and the sharing of knowledge and creativity is being heard in the west. There is no place for individualism in today's western economy and network society, and the search is on for more collective solutions.

Tex Gunning, former president of Unilever Asia, knew how to create a socially committed culture, which led to enormous growth for the company. As an entrepreneur, he saw the fight against poverty as a social duty: 'People of my generation have grown up with the idea that business is a separate part of society, indeed that society is built up of many parts. This is a total misconception which ensures a degradation of society. We all live in one world, and so the problem of poverty cannot be viewed separately. Poverty affects us all. If something is wrong in our society, we have a moral and social obligation to do something. It does not matter whether you see it as a business opportunity, a social duty or a social threat. The point is to act. And the great thing is, that the more you define your business in a social context, the more successful it will become.'
Interview with Tex Gunning, 'Poverty affects us all', posted by 1We on YouTube.[1]

[1] We (One World Experience) is a pioneering international development organisation with a corporate sector background. It tries to make a difference through innovative projects and positive television programmes.

The transition phase in which the West now finds itself offers a wonderful opportunity to clear away a lot of debris, and to prepare for a new era, where the gross national product walks hand in hand with the gross national happiness. We must grasp this opportunity with both hands. Then the West can focus clearly on sustainability. This was seen initially as a hype, with everyone voicing their own interpretation, throwing words in to justify austerity measures. However, that is already behind us. Sustainability is no longer just using less paper or maintaining CSR policy. It has become mainstream, gradually yet firmly taking root in the hearts and minds of the people. A new reference point has appeared on the horizon to lead us to a happier world.

A happier world as a focus for the green economy
Many organisations and companies have already developed numerous products and services around sustainability, arranging their internal organisation and production processes accordingly. These organisations and business are becoming part of the so-called 'green economy'. But sustainability does not necessarily lend itself to new revenue; rather it is the backbone of a better world. The green economy offers a very positive and promising contribution, but it is only a means to an end.

The West is preparing for great change, where the perception of the humanist philosophy of Ubuntu can help people and organisations pave the way to a happier world. It is therefore now high time for leaders, organisations and companies to prepare.

One example of a leader who successfully combines sustainability with profitability is Hans Wijers, former Minister of Finance and chairman of Akzo Nobel NV until early 2012. According to Maxime Verhagen, former Minister of Economic Affairs, Agriculture and

Innovation, *'Hans Wijers is a leader with a great feeling for social responsibility. He is a visionary who puts his ideas about sustainability into practice. A founder of the green economy.'* The link between economy and sustainability is a recurrent feature of Wijers' career. *'As a minister, his philosophy was that green and growth go together. As an entrepreneur, he proved that focusing on sustainable profitability can lead to groundbreaking innovations.'* See www.rijksoverheid.nl

Wijers formulated several tribal management lessons for executive leaders:

The six most important words for a manager are:
'Yes, I have made a mistake.'
The five most important words for a manager are:
'I am proud of you!'
The four most important words for a manager are:
'What do you think?'
The three most important words for a manager are:
'Can I help?'
The two most important words for a manager are:
'Thank you.'
The most important word for a manager is:
'We'.

If organisations and companies are going to function from a tribal human and world perspective, this can have a great impact. Among other things, this means that tribal values will have to become firmly embedded under the skin of the organisation, and fixed in the genes of its employees. These values must be recognisable and visible not only internally within the organisation, but also in cooperation, appreciation, objective setting, work processes, structures and systems. And such a growth process is not achieved overnight; it needs time, attention and connective leadership. It will then certainly go towards a work place with soul: a community.

Creating a work place with soul

Organisations with soul are genuine and deeply motivated. They want to create effective significance, make a difference. They have higher ideals, which inspire and direct them. They also make clear decisions, which they stick to. They do not discard their beliefs for the sake of short-term profit. They focus on constructing genuine relationships, and the desire to create value. To gain connection with their surroundings, they look within themselves, and this eventually becomes genuine. It is up to the leader to lay his soul bare in order to challenge the people to create value together.

Placing people not professionals centrally

An individualistic work place is all about 'the professional'. This term is linked to the productivity or performance which you must deliver. The professional is more than his job; he is above all someone with different roles and many experiences along the way. If an organisation is blind to this, a wealth of experience and knowledge is neglected. And this is a missed opportunity. There is therefore little sense in investing in an annual teambuilding session or 'employee of the month' campaign. Investing structurally in an employee means that you consider him as a person with many facets and qualities, and you will be able to address his full potential. This affords a great sense of appreciation. The leader who realises that he is just a cog in the wheel looks differently at people. It is no longer 'I' that is central, but 'We'. He thinks and speaks from a true 'We' perspective, where he wants only the best for his organisation and staff. So he makes considered choices. He may make mistakes, because everyone knows he is acting in the interests of the group. A leader who operates with this 'We' feeling shares responsibility with the many people around him. He is not alone. He loves his people, and they love him.

Loving people sincerely

People's behaviour is influenced by the inherent trust within a tribal organisation. They do not point to each other or wait for each other, but dare to stick their own necks out. This is appreciated, even if not always successful. Truth is a high priority for the tribal organisation, whether it brings good or bad news, both of which are equally important.

Sharing truth and good news

In traditional western organisations, one person supported by a management team usually holds the reins. This can be a lonely position for a leader. Everything is decided in closed meetings and the organisation shares only what it feels is prudent. Therefore only top-down communication for implementation exists. This is a very efficient process with regard to managing time and money, but it is not always so easy to create firm support from such an approach.

In a tribal organisation, open dialogue takes place with delegation amongst the entire company. Any advice or conclusions from this open dialogue are crucially important. The leader will listen and act accordingly, and supportively, even if it is not always good news. The communication is open and honest, and nobody withholds information.

Organising open dialogue instead of closed meetings

The West is familiar with an elaborate meetings culture, where it is possible that dilemmas do not actually reach the table. Tribal organisations are not so formal. Their gatherings are in the spirit of open dialogue, where people can discuss freely and informally. Subjects arise which would normally have to wait their turn in a business agenda. The leader regularly takes part in these informal meetings, which reinforces the bond between him and his staff.

Fewer meetings, more coffee

Western organisations and leaders certainly have their own stories, symbols and rituals. There is a large breeding ground of material which both connects and strengthens. People can identify themselves with the organisation simply through relating, conveying, nurturing and repeating these stories. They become interpreters, and behave accordingly.

Using stories, rituals and symbols

Ubuntu philosophy as a moral compass

Communicating from a single sustainability policy has become more widespread amongst organisations. They could therefore use Ubuntu philosophy as a firmly anchored moral compass. This might bring gross national happiness a little closer. Organisations could integrate tribal values into green economy initiatives, for example, which could be implemented within sectors such as government, education, healthcare and jurisdiction. These sectors would then gain a more people-oriented focus, and be better placed to realise any necessary connections on social or economic levels.

> *'But fighting or fleeing overlooks reform in structure and lifestyle. The challenge remains to actually do something, together with others and in conjunction with the whole community'*
> **Former Queen Beatrix of The Netherlands in her 2011 Christmas message**

During this transition phase, we can see many examples which indicate to organisations and companies which tribal values to assume. This is happening even at products and services level.

The cooperation is back on the agenda

Many western administrations have encouraged independent enterprise during the last twenty years. A large number of people chose, through reasons of their own, to use their knowledge and services to set up independently. So plasterers and other tradesmen bought their own vans, and started working for themselves. This put them largely on competition with each other.

These independent entrepreneurs are now in fact refocusing on complementary cooperation, and they are participating more often in collaboration. Their goal is to give, share and exchange their knowledge and services while maintaining their own identity and ability to create together. These small and medium-sized enterprises (SMEs) have become familiar because of a long need for solidarity, and they function in the same manner as modern tribal organisations.

They tend to focus on the associate value principle rather than the shareholder value. These small and medium-sized tradesmen's businesses working together participate fully in tenders from long-established companies. They do not put themselves centrally, but look at what the market needs before making their bids. They are also promising players and formidable competition because they optimise their strengths to reduce overheads.

Furthermore, freelancers do not have any substitutes. They do not simply use The New Way of Working; they really are The New Way of Working. The best available legal form for this is the old familiar cooperation.

The amount of cooperatives has grown by 25% in three years. There were 5800 registered with the Dutch Chambers of Commerce at the beginning of 2011. Two years earlier there had been 4600, 500 of whom were in the business services category (400 in 2008). Colour my Company is an example of a cooperative which connects various entrepreneurs, each of whom specialise in marketing, communication, branding, inbound marketing, corporate design, web technology and customer relations management (CRM). All these different services offered by self-employed business people ensure a rich diversity of perspectives, and a range of services. See www.colourmycompany.nl

Some experiments and pilots are already running which go somewhat beyond the listed SMEs. These are shared-value cooperatives.

'Collaboration can bring in large assignments; certainly because public procurement means that the self-employed can be left behind,' says Esther Raats, chair of the Platform Zelfstandige Ondernemers (Independent Workers). 'Purchasing regulations are so harsh that it is almost impossible to participate as a self-employed person.'

'Our experience is that a multidisciplinary approach ensures effective solutions. Tasks are not specifically allocated, but agreements are reached about the workload. If one member makes an acquisition, payment is received,' says Catja van den Broek, one of the initiators of Colour my Company. *'We want to eliminate the feeling that 'I do more than you'. It is our mission to offer collaboration in (every) service required by entrepreneurs going their own way to become distinctive and successful.'*

Tribal partnerships: give, share, exchange, create, and you will feel reconnected.

Shared-value cooperatives often arise from dissatisfaction, unrest, a desire to change and take control. They adopt cooperative thinking in order to realise their ambition. They are equipped with great knowledge, passion and an almost Robin Hood-like quality: alongside initiative, management, collaboration, transparency and ethical business, they also want to out-manoeuvre the dominant players. They go for fair distribution, and they are increasingly applying the law to their cooperatives. These then become more contemporary and desirable.

This system of local energy cooperatives has been successfully repeated 120 times in the Netherlands alone. Originally a civil participation initiative, they were established because of growing dissatisfaction and concern, also with the aim of decentralising energy supply. Entire villages and districts now know how to produce alternative energy with the help of these cooperatives. They operate with tribal mechanisms, which have strength-ened them. If these energy cooperatives gain ground – and they will – they will prove formidable competition for traditional energy companies.

Zonvogel (Sunbird) is an example of a cooperative community for sun-energy (see www.zonvogel.nl). Its members are joint owners of sun-energy installations, and the power generated by them. Each member may use or sell this energy at will. Zonvogel's objective is to contribute to a breakthrough in using the sun's energy in the Netherlands, where everyone can participate, and which is economical, ecological and profitable. There is now a new growth market in alternative cooperative energy companies.

There is a noticeable advance in the care sector, where cooperatives want to treat their clients humanely. Zorgprofessional (Care professional), a Dutch national cooperative of care workers, is one of these. It is a partnership of independent nurses and carers with a common goal: to provide proper care. The healthcare sector is undergoing enormous change. It is under pressure from market forces,
which put financial gain above quality of care. Zorgprofessional believes that the client can only rely

on quality of care if the care provider has enough time and space to fulfill this. The cooperative was established and designed by its members, the nurses and carers themselves. It is a professional and legally authorised institution meeting everyday demands.
See www.dezorgprofessional.nl

'Technology is the driving force behind new ways of organisation and collaboration. We mainly work together via the Internet: Ning as a customised network, Google Apps for (video) chat, sharing agendas, and collaborating on documents. In addition, Skype, Thymer (for project management and timekeeping) and Moneybird for invoicing.'
Allard Janssen, co-initiator of Call for Action, a full-service online business agency and SME cooperative.

The legal status of the cooperative is fitting for our new age and The New Way of Working, and is therefore back on the business agenda.

Co-creation by means other than money

The New Age is one where money will not be the only method of payment. In this transition phase, organisations are busy experimenting with alternatives. Alongside paying in euros or dollars, you can now exchange products and services. A points system offers the opportunity to barter, or accumulate. Giving and sharing leads to short or long term returning of favours. *'Time, energy or care can be earned, applied or exchanged. In line with this, any profit or gain is shared among the participants,'* according to Marloes Top, from the Radboud University of Nijmegen in the P+ journal, which carried out this study (2012) Various pilots and experiments are currently underway, one example of which is the health insurer PGGM, who allow its members to exchange 'care coins' for its services. These coins can be earned by performing voluntary work, care giving or doing chores, and can either be redeemed straightaway or put towards extra supporting care later in life. Comparable initiatives offer a high level of liberation. People feel connected, and experience a joint search for solutions and assistance as something positive.

In this transition phase, the care sector is increasingly looking for suitable models to provide more people-oriented care. The elderly and vulnerable do not want to waste away in an environment short of energy; they want to be a part of the community. They make themselves heard, and fortunately they are listened to. This explains the emergence of alternative living and working methods, care groups and care homes. In addition, cafés and shops employing the mentally handicapped, immigrants or the elderly are gaining increasing ground in this new transition phase. Here, people can work together for a good life.

The international foundation Planetree is an example of an organisation which supports health institutions by the realisation of highly valued people-oriented care in a healing environment, by a sound organisation. They take full account of the culture and context of both patients and employees. This reflects the use of tribal mechanism to enhance the happiness of everyone concerned.
In 2009, Frido Kraanen, director of Cooperation and Members of PGGM, Noor Bongers from the innovation platform Great Place to Live and Harold Smits from A-Life brought together a network of 150 participants from the elderly sector, all of whom were visionaries, daring entrepreneurs from the PGGM, Espria, Uvit,

Twijnstra Gudde and Great Place to Live. The goal was always a valuable approach to old age, with far-sighted vision and examples of business model renewal. The following text is from the introduction to the 'New Old Age' report, about the research project on the future of care, well being, living and retirement.

The world is changing. Look around you . . .

Many things change, and many things remain the same in our daily lives. People have needed to listen to music for years. That will not change quickly. It is just the form that changes in tempo: LP, cassette, CD, minidisc, MP3. You can see these kinds of developments everywhere; they are not the result of technological breakthroughs.

An undercurrent heralding a standardisation of target brands and co-creation is present in our society. Today's market leaders are not those of tomorrow. Therefore we must continue to be alert to the drive of new generations, keep an eye on business being conducted differently and listen to what clients want.

Companies want to be significant for a seemingly unfathomable group of people who swarm about in different directions. How can you make an impression on such a fluid environment? This can add value to the experience of the consumer. Your products or services will enrich his or her personal perception of life and requirements. This is useful – and it works.

Give people the chance to do something themselves with the product. Genuine communication and honesty about the product are crucial. 'Self-regulation for the elderly' is central to the New Old Age project. How can you contribute to this? How can you add value to a group of elderly people who want to mange their old age by themselves?

The choice between standard or luxury packages will remain. Consumers receive care in return for money.

But some people have no money, or they have other demands. They gather together in collectives, based on their own questions and convictions. This may or may not be apparent to providers, because people move towards an immeasurable periphery (they do not fit into a client profile). This is an interesting societal trend which indicates that times are changing, and another role for service providers is desirable.

The full report appears on www.vuconnected.nl

Continued attention to solidarity and meaning is an important aspect of Ubuntu. You cannot start too soon. Western secondary schools have recently been actively involving children in voluntary work, to show them the pleasure and value in contributing to their surroundings. Pupils have begun to study this social stage as part of their curriculum. Teenagers are learning to make their environment significant, which has an impact for them, at a time when their personal identity is developing.

There are many more initiatives in the name of co-creation, where access instead of possession is central. This access is then shared with others. Community values such as respect and trust, courage and enterprise, humanity and appreciation form the basis of lasting optimal collaboration and services, high quality and social engagement. Only then can community members be successful in the long term.

Tribal industry

Tribal communities have become more important and more powerful than ever in this time of co-creation. They increasingly determine people's identity in their private lives and work situations. There is a greater need for enhancing one's identity, conveyed through rituals, codes, clothes etc. It is a logical step for a whole tribal industry to develop around these communities, which knows how to nurture and fulfill identity requirements.

Tribal marketing is soaring now, in order to reach these communities. The Internet with its free, accessible and global communication plays a great role here. Social media like Twitter, blogs and YouTube have added completely new dimensions to tribal communities, and illustrate the importance of belonging.

The Ubuntu software house is a fine example. It has a contact office in London, but operates chiefly via the Internet. It has created a network for developers and users that functions as a tribal community, from the viewpoint that software should be freely available worldwide. Everyone is welcome to take part. The enthusiasm for this of thousands of experts across the world, and the passionate use of it by others, has delivered a wealth of data, knowledge and information, which leads in turn to new services. Giving is therefore receiving. The company successfully uses tribal marketing to reach, support, maintain and enlarge its Ubuntu community. Its business conduct clearly shows Ubuntu principles. A quick look at their site, www.ubuntu.com, is interesting for everybody, whether interested in IT or not. It displays a thoroughly modern form of giving, sharing and creating.
South African millionaire Mark Shuttleworth is the big chief of the software house.

'It is an indescribable honour to work for this company. Higher profit or market-shares are not my objective; nobody wants this any more. I want to leave a better world behind, set up a new business model, make a difference, collaborate, and not stand on the sideline. I can do this most effectively at Unilever.'

Paul Polman, Unilever, 2011

'I cannot do very much as chairman. I need specialists within the company who can do more in their field than I can. My job is really ensuring that everyone can achieve success here. Harry Truman once said, "You can achieve anything in life if you don't mind who gets the credits." We need a responsible growth model, with the emphasis on the long term and a feeling of collaboration. Unilever has such a tradition. Values are returning. Short-term gain does not benefit society. That would be stealing from our children and grandchildren.'

Paul Polman, Unilever, 2011

Innovation models for a happier world
Business is increasingly searching for a happier world.

Paul Polman is the CEO of Unilever, one of the largest food enterprises in the world. 163,000 employees call him 'boss'. With the slogan 'small actions, big difference', Unilever has undergone huge transformation in areas of health, well-being, sustainability and value creation, due to his inspirational leadership. Unilever wants to halve CO2 emissions, water usage and rubbish mountains by 2020. This includes the whole chain from raw materials to end product. Meanwhile, they also want to double turnover. This is all in the knowledge that consumers do not want to pay more for sustainable products. Given that people can access Unilever products worldwide, the impact will be enormous. This model commands respect and imitation. The full interview with Paul Polman is available to read on the VNO-NCW website: www.vno-ncw.nl/publicaties.

A particular business in Rwanda, on the African continent, should not escape mention in the light of innovative models. Urwibutso, located in the Nyirangarama region in Rwanda, is the concern of Mr. Sina Gérard. Gérard has taken this underprivileged area as the starting point for all his business activities. It now employs around 2000 people and wins international prizes for its creation.

Urwibutso: a business empire based on community involvement

One of the most engaging entrepreneurs that I have had the pleasure of meeting in the last few years is Mr. Sina Gérard from Rwanda. He has successfully established companies which contribute to the well-being and happiness of his hometown, Nyirangarama.

After being raised in a farming family, he noticed the difficulties his parents, like so many others, had with selling grain in the local market. To help his parents, and to earn a living for himself, he started baking bread rolls, which he sold in a small local shop. He quickly became well known for his snacks, drizzled with locally produced chilli sauce. This publicity led to a demand for the chilli sauce, and Mr. Sina Gérard saw an opportunity: he started producing and exporting industrial quantities under the brand name 'Akabaga Chilli Sauce'.

Mr. Sina Gérard saw the impact of this first success on his hometown; it gained a reputation which made its inhabitants and farmers proud of their surroundings and products. The town developed into a tourist attraction with a restaurant, shops, music and dance. The opportunity to create new products like banana wine, beer and pineapple juice for export, arose through visionary investment in better quality seeds and the introduction of unfamiliar fruit such as grapes, apples, pineapples and strawberries. The seeds and fertilizers were freely distributed among the farmers, and Mr. Gérard provided free training and assistance. A farmers' cooperation was established with more than 750 members and contracts drawn up for guaranteed supply and procurement. Everybody could therefore contribute to the area's development. Mr. Sina Gérard introduces one new product a year onto the market through his company Urwibutso, which now boasts a wide diversity of products, and the town is no longer dependent on only a few. He imported the bets cows imaginable from the Netherlands, and built Rwanda's largest pigsty. As a result of this success, the government tackled the infrastructure to and from the town: the main road from Kigali, the capital, to the tourist resort of Gisenyi passes Mr. Sina Gérard's town with good reason, with optimal access leading to yet greater success. Mr. Gérard has also built a school for more than 500 students, not only to offer an education to his employees' children, but also because he wants better-educated employees in his companies.

Now that the reputation of the town is assured and the infrastructure improved, Mr. Sina Gérard can see an opportunity for eco-tourism. He wants to introduce agro-tourism among the vineyards on one of the hills. He is tapping into arable and livestock for a completely new market. He consciously chooses to continue investing in his hometown, since as he says, 'How could it be otherwise? I choose to do everything, because I am here and I can do it.' This makes him revered and supported by the whole community. Of course, his visionary leadership and effective entrepreneurship are essential in achieving results, but what lies at the root of this success is the feeling of pride and happiness enjoyed by the community, where everyone works together to build a new future and Mr. Gérard has won his position.

Léon van Rijckevorsel, co-founder GreenDreamCompany

The whole world can take notice of Mr. Sina Gérard's special approach, his success, and his passionate and engaging leadership. His company could be an example for western environments that are not doing so well at the moment.

These developments all need nurturing and knowledge, The Erasmus University of Rotterdam, The Netherlands, began a new initiative in the spring of 2012: Erasmus Institute for Happiness Economics Research Organisation (EHERO). This institute deals with the measurability and comprehension of 'happiness' with the study of 'happiness economics.' There is even a 'world happiness database' with figures which measure the contentment felt in people's lives in 149 different countries. Wealth does not seem to be the overriding factor. Ruut Veenhoven, professor Emeritus of social conditions for human happiness, is director of the 'World Database of Happiness', founder of the 'Journal of Happiness Studies' and advisor Happiness Indicator. He is known as the 'happy professor'. He gave the following answer to the question 'Can organisations contribute to the happiness of their employees?' during an interview with Auke Brouwer on www.acta.nl

'There is no single recipe for the whole organisation. The rubbish collector's circumstances are different from a trainee dentist's, but you can still monitor their happiness. Research shows that people generally feel more comfortable at home than at work. And this difference in feeling between work and home life really says more than current work satisfaction surveys. The Happiness Indicator measures this difference efficiently. An organisation can use the information to make their staff happier. And being happy has a positive effect on work productivity. Happiness is really a biological signal: things are going well for you. The downside: you become less careful. Perhaps you should not be too happy about taking on tasks such as accountancy, for example, but you certainly can for jobs with a strongly social component. Happiness is infectious.

Professor of happiness Ruut Veenhoven, 2012

EHERO's ambition is to make use of research and policy support to transform the gross national product into 'gross national happiness'. New initiatives and business models are consciously engaging in the creation of complex values around nature, environment, care, attention and money, all striving together for a happier world. These are beautiful, optimistic and very important, because they are based on giving, sharing, exchanging and creating, completely open in character and worthy of imitation.

International work and business in a happy world

By formulating responses to big themes, these initiatives and business models are appropriately using collaboration across the borders of surrounding organisations and countries. Information and communication technology offer helpful new opportunities. Pricing has changed. Technical advancements such as Skype, mail and mobile banking are fully available in rising economies, and make working internationally much easier.

It is increasingly important to link one's own knowledge and creativity with others. This means that people will invest more in finding connections with other communities, being open to other cultures, and being quick to create new links. Then they will be able to connect their own concerns and context with those of others, and will be as interested in other people as in their own tribal community.

International business could not happen without awareness of the context of your partners. You immerse yourself in other cultures, explore qualities and learn values which are important in creating a happier world. As children from two worlds, 'diasporas' form an important link, in this perspective.

Diasporas as a unique international selling point

Many African countries work to encourage their foreign diasporas to either return home or invest in their homeland. This is happening on a large scale. Because of the western crisis, many Africans are returning home. In many cases, they set up business with family members, which has lead to a rise in small and medium enterprises on the African continent. This is advantageous to western companies active abroad or considering it. It is easier to do business with someone who understands and has networks in both cultures. Diasporas are invaluable to the new world.

There are still more interesting developments. Much has been invested in the education of African students by collaborative development programmes. Nuffic, a Dutch organisation for international cooperation in higher education, has given the most talented students the chance of an international education. They are now working hard to develop their homeland, and they have not forgotten the opportunities offered to them by the West. Furthermore, they have established valuable and friendly relations during their studies abroad. These new friendships and contacts ensure a high business reward factor. The Chinese, who also conduct business, in Africa do not take advantage of this aspect, but the West can certainly make better use of it.

Concluding remarks

The key to success in a happier world lies in forming tribal communities not only in Africa,but also in western organisations. Inspiration will play a big part in organisations, as well as products and services. Tribal approaches will also shape the future on an international level. The big global questions which demand answers must be treated globally. All attention will be on collaboration and communication. The power of diasporas as a link in this process is invaluable.

The following chapter offers a glimpse into the heart of the GreenDreamCompany: a western company, active within the African market. It shows how a western organisation is trying to integrate the philosophy of Ubuntu into its daily business and international projects.

Best Practice: GreenDreamCompany

'The only true voyage of discovery would not be to visit new landscapes but to possess other eyes'

M. Proust (1871-1922)

GreenDreamCompany is an example of a western company aiming to put Ubuntu values into practice. Its founders and directors are Léon van Rijckevorsel and Leontine van Hooft, author of this book. It is a young family business, built on Ubuntu values. Integrity forms the basis of every activity, whether in relation to the people with whom we collaborate, or the projects that we realise.

We first encountered Ubuntu ten years ago in our former business, where African people in The Netherlands crossed our path. We were wonder-struck, we wanted more extensive knowledge, and so we attended masterclasses held by the South African professor Lovemore Mgibi. His work in translating Ubuntu into organisation frameworks and leadership philosophy is impressive. We were convinced that our work would become more enjoyable through Ubuntu.

Once at work on the African continent, we quickly recognised what drove the people with whom we were working, why they acted as they did, and what we could suitably expect. Westerners do not always find this easy; in Africa, hospitality is more important than agenda management, for example. In some African countries, you do not make appointments weeks beforehand. You come along, and are helped on the spot, or receive an answer not much later. You would only be unsuccessful if someone is called away. This happened to us regularly, which we found difficult, at first, being such slaves to our schedules. However, it taught us to loosen up and work more creatively. Admittedly, that sometimes meant taking a nearly empty agenda on a business trip, hoping simply to meet up with each other. But that also meant that you were always welcome, and would be given all the time and attention necessary for the subject in question.

We have made many African and western friends through Ubuntu. It is in fact impossible to go to the African continent only to do business. We have found this very enjoyable, as we like investing in contact with people. The division between work and private life becomes therefore smaller, because we have the feeling of being less occupied with working.

We certainly have not changed tack as far as our business is concerned; far from it. Connecting the best of both worlds is an art. This means we have fewer meetings, and a looser schedule than before. The character of these meetings has also changed, because we simply sit down and start talking.

We started by looking at what we could do differently. I will describe what this means in practice for our organisation in this chapter.

What does the organisation stand for? What is the product? How does Ubuntu translate within the organisation? What does this mean for our employees? What does it require of them? How is Ubuntu visible in projects? What does the organisation come up against? What recommendations are there for others interested in Ubuntu? This chapter offers a glimpse into the heart of GreenDreamCompany, and answers all these questions.

The nautilus shell logo

The nautilus shell is a beautiful representation of infinity in eternity. If you open the nautilus shell, you will see a spiral. A very special process has gone on here. The creature starts off very small, and builds new shell chambers around itself with every lunar phase. These chambers form a spiral, which artists and architects have used as a golden mean for centuries. The nautilus shell is a perfect illustration of connectivity, so it is the perfect logo for us, because it absolutely represents our ideals. It is a symbol of harmonic balance between being and becoming – of Ubu and Ntu.

What drives GreenDreamCompany?

GreenDreamCompany specialises in developing tourist areas in emerging African markets. It is the result of various considerations, and so therefore a well-informed decision. The founders' professional background includes project development and management, and organisation anthropology. They felt the need to connect this with their passion and fascination for cultural travel and heritage. At the same time, their new insights into collaborative development take on board the position of tourism, and opportunities for entrepreneurship on the African continent, which are relevant to even small western organisations.jding.

The role and impact of tourism is gaining recognition. G20 is a group of ninety European Union countries. They want to be a forum for collaboration and discussion in the field of international finance. During their annual conference on 18 – 19 June 2012, the G20 world leaders

'We commend the G20 world leaders for recognising the importance of Travel & Tourism as a driver of economic growth and job creation for the first time and stand ready to support all efforts by the G20 summits in this respect. This is a significant success for the industry and could not have happened without the support of President Calderón, a leader who truly understands the socio-economic value of tourism and its potential to create new jobs in such difficult economic times, and without the commitment of Secretary Gloria Guevara, who so successfully chaired the T20 (Tourism Ministers of G20 countries) last month. Mexico is an example in marketing its extraordinary tourism destinations but also in tourism policy namely through significant advances in visa policies which encourage more inbound tourists.'

'By facilitating visas, the G20 countries stand to gain five million jobs at a time of rampant unemployment across the world. These are in addition to the hundreds of millions of direct and indirect jobs already being supported every day by the sector.'

Taleb Rifai, Secretary General of the UNWTO, and David Scowsill, president and CEO of WTTC, in answer to the 2012 G20 manifesto

recognised for the first time the influential role of travel and tourism as the driving force behind job creation, economic growth and the fight against poverty.

The impact of tourism is very large, not only for work opportunities and a country's image, but also in the field of gender equality, agriculture, education and healthcare. Sustainable tourism development makes it possible to protect nature and culture, and to fund conservation.

Tourism can also be powerful with regard to a country's political stability. For example, when people were advised against traveling to Kenya due to internal conflict in 2011, the whole sector, from airlines and hotel-owners to tour-guide organisations, was able to successfully put pressure on the government to reach a rapid resolution.

The Peace Park Foundation is another good example of creating stability. These are nature parks or reserves, created at the meeting points of the borders between three or four countries. They form a stabilising zone between these countries and provide nature preservation. Tourists have the unique opportunity to enjoy nature and culture in such a way that they can have breakfast in South Africa, lunch in Botswana and dinner in Zimbabwe.

There is still more: tourism allows an area's inhabitants to take pride in what they are. They rediscover their natural habitat through the tourist's admiration. This leads to a new realisation that strengthens

empowerment and stimulates entrepreneurship. The fact that such a positive business climate exists, with such a great working potential, means that foreign and diaspora investors dare to settle in the country. Tourism is therefore an enormous catalyst in creating work opportunities beyond its own boundaries.

In short, GreenDreamCompany has deliberately chosen to be a business where great significance and impact for people and nature play a large part. This means that our mission is strong and powerful.

What does GreenDreamCompany do?

Our product has grown over the years from the development and establishment of small-scale eco-resorts in as yet undiscovered beautiful locations, to a much broader concept. Ubuntu philosophy is increasingly important. We realise that we can only build and operate ecologically if the setting is suitable. If the area is not central, we have to fly in a great deal of food and materials, which overshoots our sustainable goal in a very costly manner. In addition, we do not want to build yet another beautiful but totally isolated resort. We want our resorts to be meeting places for the community, where guests can easily walk into the village for shopping and local contact. We also want to create jobs, directly and indirectly.

This means that as far as possible, we employ local entrepreneurs, farmers and fishermen. They are the success behind the resort, which in turn forms the basis of their own success. It can be that quality of the local

'It is our ambition to establish 10,000 jobs in the next few years, and to create magnificent places for cultures to embrace each other'

produce and supply is not good enough, which means nothing to the discerning tourist, who wants good service, comfortable bed, delicious food in a beautifully maintained location with a wonderful view. This requires a well-oiled and sustainable supply value chain with regard to building and transport, food, equipment, souvenirs, crafts etc. This is why we want to work to develop supply value chains, to operate a successful resort in a promising, beautiful and caring environment. It will not only be stones that are central to the project, but also people. They alone can allow the stones to flourish.

Who are the clients?

GreenDreamCompany's most important clients are, amongst others, local and international investors and part-ners, African and western business administrations with special interests in collaborative development, individual purchasers of the cottages, the eco-resort operators, and eventually the tourists. They are all aware that Ubuntu is the under-lying philosophy to our working methods.

What is the approach?

The five P's: People, Planet, Profit, Pleasure and Passion
GreenDreamCompany werkt 'van nature' volgens de princi-pes die zijn samengevat in de vijf P's. Het zit in ons DNA!

GreenDreamCompany works according to the principles summarised in the five P's. It is inherent in our DNA!

People: because we love people and are always looking for the best result. Therefore we take into account everyone concerned, all our GreenDreamers, our partners and rela-tions, and everyone working on our projects. This means that we demand high standards of performance delivery and quality of dedication on one hand, yet also developing

ideas together to make our work as pleasant as possible. For example, we aim for a 32-hour working week for every-one, because we feel that the balance between four days at work and three days off is perfect.

Planet: because we realise that we need the earth, not the other way around. We are guests on the earth, and should conduct ourselves with respect accordingly.

Therefore, GreenDreamCompany works with the following ten criteria:
1. The project must be appropriate to the natural environ-ment. The landscape is the leader.
2. Any building depends on the surroundings.
3. We always select natural, lasting and strong material, making as much use as possible of what is already avail-able in and around the location.
4. We help protect nature, and maximise its potential if necessary.
5. We use sustainable energy.
6. We use water responsibly
7. There is no contamination at all.
8. Good employment and entrepreneurship translates into job creation, education, healthcare and gender equality.
9. The safety of employees, communities and tourists must be guaranteed.
10. We cooperate with governments, the private sector, NGO's and research institutes.

We are gradually applying The New Way of Working: reimbursing travel costs, working from home, Skyping to avoid unnecessary travel, encouraging the use of public transport and bicycles, and putting on an extra jumper when it is cold. Our tourist projects are working towards sustainability in our supply value chains. We encourage farmers, businesses and other suppliers in the chains to work sustainably.

Profit: because a healthy company must be financially sustainable for its future existence. Our tourist projects are also based on business operations. Thriving projects help us to realise other projects with more employment opportunities and greater impact.

Passion: because this is just how we work, using our heads, hearts and hands. GreenDreamers are 100% behind our products and services, which helps us to continue where others leave off. We are involved!

Pleasure: because this is what we want for others and ourselves, and also because it is what tourism stands for.

Leadership at GreenDreamCompany

You are part of a team as a leader, not in a higher position. Without the team there would not be any leadership. Everyone in the team has his or her own role. This means that a GreenDreamCompany leader is also an active team member, a double role, as it were, not only because we are a small company, but also because we also believe that a leader should keep both feet on the ground. It is a basic error to limit yourself to leadership. We do not appreciate a distant leader, so in this sense we are a one level organisation.

As a leader, you display yourself and your vulnerability. Recognising the quality of others sometimes means that you have no actual understanding, only reliance on their insight and qualities. It is sometimes simply a question of seeing together why people do not achieve something instead of impatiently taking work back. Someone can often make progress by tackling a problem when there is more light and energy. Leadership also means that you make extraordinary efforts to try and inspire others, even on a bad day. But sometimes intervention is necessary if something is not going well, or not running smoothly. Leadership is having respect for others, and challenging people. Being respectful to others ensures that you will also be treated with respect. It is a privilege to be a leader and part of a team like ours. The GreenDreamCompany leaders are also its founders. This aspect, combined with our style of leadership, what and how we perform, creates a narrative which exists all around us. People are curious about our working methods, our approach and business dealings on the African continent. We are regularly asked to speak, which we gladly do. We are thrilled with the interest and the publicity, which helps us in the attention we give to our projects, philosophy and Africa.

Pride in our global team

We look – genuinely interested – at our team members, and see beyond their professionalism. We become deeply involved in people as humans. They are extremely valuable to us, so we prefer not to use the word 'professional', which only describes a part of somebody, as if the rest is unimportant or hardly worth mentioning. You do not need an annual performance appraisal or a performance review planned weeks in advance to find out how somebody is. We have hardly ever organised formal discussions here. But if something is important, the door is always open. We have time for a chat, to ask how things are going, think about personal dilemmas. We try to contribute to solutions without taking over the problem, so that we remain up-to-date with our people's domestic situation, which in turn has an indirect effect on GreenDreamCompany.

People are associated in everything about our company. We consider problems together. It can be astounding how you can reach a solution and creativity together with an open attitude and dialogue. The best ideas often come from unexpected quarters. We value not only the best idea, but also the fact that people actively put their heads together.

We see diversity as a richness. A global team is evenly built on people of both sexes, various ages, and cultural backgrounds. We harness the value that flows from this. We do not, of course, pass over things which are going less well, we fix them together. Somebody might on one hand have to use a Dutch spell check programme, while on the other hand be perfectly at home with training people in the English language Customer Relation Management system.

Benefiting from our team's diversity means that we have more knowledge, experience and a broader in-house network, than if we only appealed to the professional side of people.

From work experience venue to ambassadorship.
There are many people at the moment who are having difficulty finding work in their field. Others would like the chance to change jobs, but are unable to find suitable employment in these difficult times. The founders of GreenDreamCompany have also been in the same situation, and know from experience what a testing time this can be.

GreenDreamCompany now offers permanent work experience placements. People have the opportunity to

'My formal title is Management Assistant. But I do much more than that. For example, my own cultural background helps me with the 'Working crossing borders' training, which people do with us before they start work in Africa. Ethiopia recently presented its own classification system, developed for the hotel sector. It was simply its own star system, not available in English, only in the national language, Amharic. I had no problems translating this into Dutch and English, so we were able to quickly pass on guidelines to the local architect and instruct the local building contractor.'
Almaz Merha, Management Assistant at GreenDreamCompany

make a career change. They often come from completely different cultural organisations or jobs, and they are now looking for more meaningful work, either reflecting on their work process, or gaining experience in a more international context to enhance their CV's. Working with our team teaches people how to apply their knowledge, create new insights and skills, and make contact with a new network.

GreenDreamCompany has paid staff, interns and people in transition phases working together on projects. We give them all the same counselling, and make the same demands of them, which fulfill our theme of giving, sharing and creating. They sometimes find employment, or a place in the network, or become self-employed, but collaboration is nearly always the key to a kind of ambassadorship.

Coffee and mint tea break

Last year, GreenDreamCompany discontinued the traditional meetings system, because we found it more effective and pleasant to meet over a cup of coffee or mint tea. Everyone always brings a notebook, and every issue is treated on its own merits.

'Our cleaning lady is of Moroccan-Turkish origin. When her daughter was getting married, all the ladies from our team were invited to the bride's evening, full of song and delicious food. According to Berber tradition, her brothers were the only men allowed. The bridegroom and his family arrived at the end of the evening, which was very ceremonial. This was an impressive and unforgettable experience for everyone present, not least for us ladies, as the bridal pair were quite westernised, and had lived together for a while.

This informality means that we get to know each other very well, learn a lot from each other, and answer all our questions. After the break, people only need a few words to carry out their tasks and plan their work with each other. Everybody joins the table to discuss current issues, even the cleaning lady. Although she felt a little awkward at first, as a child of three cultures she seemed to understand cultural differences very perceptively, and had a great sense of humour.

Transparency and success

It has become much easier to share matters which need attention with each other, and to find solutions together because of people's strong commitment to their work and their open communication. Nobody withdraws. The only condition is that information should be honest and transparent. We think every success is worth celebrating, either with a compliment, or cake, champagne for one or a soft drink for another. Our success is in working to connect and stay connected. In fact, we have created our own tribal community.

Sometimes it does not work

Despite GreenDreamCompany's working methods, the subject of every interview, something might occasionally go wrong in daily practice. Interacting with each other as

'My year at GreenDreamCompany greatly helped me in my quest for a career. A refreshing look at the world, working with passion, standing for something, and going for it all contributed to my next step. It was an honour for me to be able to work with the company. My journey continues...'

Lianne Dijkstra, now employed as a consultant at Public Impact

we do, demands a lot of new colleagues, especially those with a more individualistic tendency.

Personal performance is not as important as 'we', the team. We ask people to think about the organisation in broader terms, in order to achieve a feeling of togetherness in all our business activities. People should be able to combine their knowledge and values with those of others. This demands maximum dedication, vulnerability and courage. Colleagues also discuss things which are not going so well, because somebody will be able to help. However this does not always work, in spite of everyone's best efforts and intentions, and the people concerned may take their leave of us within a year. There is no mutual feeling of success. Such experiences ensure that fewer people join directly from 'outside', and more stay with us via a work experience placement.

Small is strong

We know we are small, and therein lies our strength in creating and managing every necessary alliance. Strong and loyal partnerships add to our value, as we always have experts around us who strive with us to achieve results of the highest quality. We build a suitable concept for each project, and visualise what is necessary to realise it, as each one has different additives and ingredients. But we always use only what can be supplied locally. A team can alter the composition of a project. The starting point is to know what local knowledge and opportunities are available to use and enhance, if necessary. What the local environment cannot provide, we supplement with western knowledge and dedication. These people are part of the network around us and do not need to appear on the payroll, because it might impede our flexibility. So our starting points are often in tandem with local complementary experience and knowledge. One example of this is a western landscape architect collaborating with an African architect, or a western expert in sustainable building working with a local contractor. In this way we are sure to have the best people, and are well placed to realise big projects – without the usual associated overheads.

The Green Square methodology

In GreenDreamCompany, we work to develop tourist areas by following the 'Green Square' methodology. This means that we work in collaboration with governments, educational institutes and NGO's to enable an area to grow and flourish sustainably. The underlying philosophy is one of achieving results together, rather than individually. The following example shows this in practice.

Tribal collaboration at project level

In our view, collaboration and support for local inhabitants is a condition of success. This is also relevant at project level. From the very first day we consult the local community and immerse ourselves in the project. We hold information-groups and discuss our plans openly with community advisors. We learn more about their traditions and bring them into contact with western ones. We learn from each other. Respect and cooperation are the highest priorities, and are the most important reasons why we gladly work with local investors and partnerships. They are the ones who help us to become familiar with the local culture and circumstances, and who take the lead. We celebrate everything worth celebrating with the communities. In Ethiopia, this means that at the start of the building phase of Gorgora Nova Rock Resort on Lake Tana, there is a joint ceremony where the first stone of red earth is consecrated by the priests of the Christian Coptic Orthodox church, in the presence of the district governor, Ethiopian bank representatives and the national press. Everything concludes with a large celebration, where according to

Gorgora Eco-Village

'We have identified ten criteria for sustainable development in the Gorgora community area with our Ethiopian business partner Yemane Kokobé. The community itself took these directives to the government of Ethiopia', with the result that it was designated a new 'tourism destination' instead of 'rural area'. They called the project, 'From Gorgora Forgotten City into Gorgora Eco-Village.' The result was that the area became eligible for road paving, electricity installation and water provision. In addition, mobile phone coverage was available throughout the area.

Our Ethiopian partner is the director of the (Private) Tsedale Nega College. Due to the fact that he is a diaspora himself, lived and studied for years in Amsterdam, his Dutch network is in good shape. He and a small Dutch NGO, Alice O, set up a project for his town with the help of a Dutch subsidy, 'Gondar on the move'. Various Dutch educational institutes are linked with this project: Friesland College and the Dutch Foundation for Training Companies and Installation Work. Their students are either interns in the project, or conducting research. Tsedale Nega College has therefore been able to offer many jobless young people from the town a basic education in construction and technology. They still lack a complete education and work experience, however, so we are setting up a student building site at the Gorgora Nova Rock Resort to further educate a great number of these young people. A Dutch private initiative has made it possible for students to receive a toolbox along with their final certificate, provided by among others Gered Gereedschap, a Dutch voluntary organisation which collects tools for use in developing countries. Because they have their own tools, the market value of these young people greatly increases. We have placed them with local contractors and set up a students' building site where they can learn more before moving onto a professional building site. So we have achieved a wonderful result through working together.'

Léon van Rijckevorsel,
co-founder GreenDreamCompany

local custom, a sheep is slaughtered and eaten. This is a very important seal of cooperation.

Storytelling today

GreenDreamCompany makes extensive use of storytelling. We do this in various different ways. We broadcast our stories via newsletters, weblogs, Twitter and Facebook. We take part in competitions and make use of free publicity. We publicise our work, and cooperate with university research and publications about inspiring, sustainable and innovative entrepreneurship with others. We give master classes and lectures and are guest speakers at events. We are wholly focused on every job, internship and work experience placement, which we communicate via www. oneworld.nl. This is not just a website, simply our most active and suitable platform, which generates a lot of response and traffic for us. It is important that our communication runs smoothly.

We are even writing our own book on the philosophy behind our work, and how it can inspire people in this particularly enervating time. We reach our clients through choosing a different approach, social media, the Internet, traditional media and direct contact. Our storytelling is therefore the mechanism, as it were, inside our 'brand'.

How does storytelling work at project level?

Storytelling works no differently at project level. An entire cultural and literary study precedes the particular subject of construction. We can trace stories which are part of the environment. Every project tells its own

story, about the area's history, nature, the realisation process of the resort, the people working there and with whom we are connected by the supply value chain. During the construction phase, we communicate the story on Facebook, for example www.facebook.com/ gorgoranovarockresort. This means that we do not only reach our clients through storytelling, but we also ensure that the project enjoys maximum support in the area.

CSR and Together-4-Better Expeditions

Even though we are a small company, we work with a Corporate Social Responsibility (CSR) policy. In a company based on Ubuntu principles, this should not be necessary. Effective entrepreneurship is simply the norm, and we have decided to underscore issues further. This has to do with the fact that CSR is not common in every company. As a result, the government, for example, is required to implement CSR in tender procedures.

GreenDreamCompany has its own CSR programme, Together-4-Better Expeditions. This programme enables us to offer western people with at least five years' work experience the opportunity to internationalise their CV's, or stepping back into the work process. Well-educated people take part as well, however, because they just want to do something significant, and gladly use their holiday for it. After thorough preparation in the Netherlands, they receive a local case study submitted at one of our development areas, which they have to tackle with the guidance of a local professional or agent. An example of an individual expedition appears on the following page.

This programme delivers a win-win situation. The western client gets the chance of international work experience, or to carry out a personal CSR policy.

African organisations working on this programme gain western impulses and practical expertise. The impact of the expedition on tourism development in the area will only be measurable after a long time. For GreenDreamCompany, this means that we create support with this programme. We build our network in the area concerned, bringing both quality and knowledge to the sector, and then tourism can get underway. In fact we are a part of the area's development before the resort is even open.
 The report below from one of the programme's participants in Ethiopia highlights very well that a short expedition can set a great deal in motion.

Dear Harry,
Thank you for your remarkable commitment and devotion you have shown us in planning and achieving our marketing goal. Now we have the blue print how to organize ourselves and develop our service quality and maximize our business by putting different long- and short-term business plans. Most of all you have shown us the direction and how important teamwork is in achieving maximum tourist flow in our town. Now the wake-up call is already given and everybody should stick to the plan, now you have shown us the first steps, so we have to work in our level best. Finally I would like to thank you on behalf of Gondar city and Taye Hotel for your unforgettable and positive advices. We always look forward to have you with us.

Best regards,
Michael Hailu, Manager Taye Hotel, Gondar, Ethiopia

'The first employees at Gorgora Nova Resort were our security guards. They were so proud of their job and company T-shirts that they wanted to be the first to appear on our Facebook page. Locally recruited builders quickly followed suit. Visitors and inhabitants, Ethiopian origin diasporas and nature lovers all posted on this page. They all contributed to the birth of . . . this project.'

Léon van Rijckevorsel, co-founder GreenDreamCompany

'Gondar has a great deal to offer, but what is potentially of interest to tourists has not yet been recognised, is often fragmented and any information about it is scarcely known. In other words, tourists do not know what they are missing. I have a group of stakeholders who understand that cooperation is the only solution here. We have established the Gondar Taskforce to represent them all, and who are devoted to the joint concern of promoting the area. The group has immediately begun to collect available information, the first step in cooperation which also leads to mutual trust. Then the Taskforce can get on with all the necessary promotional activities on my blueprint. In a third phase, the Taskforce, as proposed, wants to begin research into the wishes of the visitors, the joint development of training programmes regarding tourist information facilities, developing new visitor activities, and setting up a joint lobby for the local government about amenities and infrastructure. I have had the chance to explain the various activities to the local professionals, and indicated how these can be realised in practice. I wanted to get the ball rolling, and for it to continue rolling after I left.'

Harry Bijl, independent public relations and marketing consultant

(for more information about this case, see www.harrybijl.nl)

Finding a budget in times of crisis

GreenDreamCompany's founders established the company with their own capital. We started the project in addition to the current work of our other companies at the time, because we knew that creating a genuine cash flow would take some time, owing to the character of our projects and the way we like to organise them. Another important point was that we were reluctant to develop our concept under financial pressure, which might have pushed us into making concessions.

The concept of our organisation and area developments are ongoing. We are more than active full-time employees in GreenDreamCompany. It is more important right now than at the beginning of the project to avoid getting into debt. GreenDreamCompany is, like any other, trying to make its capital grow, in order to realise the ultimate dream of a chain of beautifully sustainable areas of development on the African continent — good for both people and nature. This quest is not currently running with the aid of western banks, that is certain. African banks give us more attention.

Regarding finance, stay with the concept
Africa is becoming popular with investors. We delight in the fact that our projects, however embraceable, revel in a great deal of interest in this respect. As an investor, you always have something fun to share at a birthday party with photographs of our project on your mobile phone. However, we have also paid our dues, because if investors cannot work within our philosophy, it is difficult to respect and understand each other's objectives. Yield from our projects means that an investor should think not only in terms of financial return, but also social and ecological return.

It is sometimes impossible to be reconciled with investors' objectives, which then means that we focus on what we call impact investors. They aspire to a balance between financial and social return on investment. It is very pleasing to notice that they become personally involved in this focus. This is something which we applaud. We welcome their involvement and effort, as our projects become more concrete.

Recommendations to third parties

Ubuntu philosophy lends itself perfectly to an organisational culture as a suitable model for our times. It is also very useful for organisations that collaborate across borders with collective cultures, if only to learn how things are with the lives and work of international partners. GreenDreamCompany sees the combination of its own organisation and its projects as its greatest challenge. We experience success and pleasure in our daily work.
There are however some recommendations for people and organisations who are considering working with this philosophy, based on our experience, and this way of cooperation. They are listed below.

■ Know where to begin. Choosing this work method means opting for a different way of life particularly for people who originate from an individual culture. This is not confined to the office; it strongly influences

Finding money to invest to invest in your plans is one thing, but finding the right sort of money is quite another.

your thoughts, affects your whole operation, and also your private life. It is not choosing the path of least resistance; we experience personal growth and enrichment in our lives and work.

*Think about how you are as a leader. Are you strong and balanced enough to dare to perform with passion and carry people along with you? Are you strong enough to realise your vulnerabilities? Are you strong enough to embark together with your team? Do you understand the stories around you, and can you also lead your own life? If you truly are, then you have found a fantastic mission and job. You have set wheels in motion.

■ Be clear about the desired value of your work. Working according to Ubuntu philosophy means working from a people-oriented philosophy with space for meaning and significance. Some may call this 'soft' in today's individualistic world, perhaps associated with affordability or even something for nothing. Working with this philosophy is not soft or cheap, but strong, powerful and high quality. Be clear about this from the beginning.

■ Green Square partners should become better attuned. The Green Square methodology is an attractive one for projects – tourist area development, in our case –having maximum impact on all concerned. It also fits very well with Ubuntu philosophy. We notice every day that we are at the forefront of this development and practice. We are convinced about the value and impact of working according to this methodology, even if it is difficult to manage. Some aspects demand special attention.

Ngo's
The government is increasingly commissioning NGO's to collaborate within enterprise. This allows them to change from counselor to social partner, which we believe is a good development. They are financed through government subsidies and their own means, provided by market donors. NGO's are in competition with each other. Subsidies may only be requested twice a year, which is not always consistent with the aspirations of a company, who want to enable things more quickly. They know they can usually only persuade large public donations in times of shortages, poverty, destruction or natural disasters. A company is willing to take a chance. If no subsidy is granted, or they do not receive enough money from the market, they will not be in a position to work on a project. They will be unable to provide their contribution. We consider this to be a missed opportunity. NGO's are financed in a complex manner which does not correspond with the speed of action familiar to a company. In order to remain full Green Square partners, the financing of NGO's needs real attention.

Educational institutes
Many educational institutes have a consultancy department or business association (BV) which would gladly be connected to Green Square-based projects. They are happy to offer students work experience. We find this entirely feasible if their participation in a project is practical. This is not always the case, unfortunately. However, focusing on practical applied research can be successful. We would appreciate educational institutes discontinuing fixed internships, because this creates more opportunities for students

Governments
Governments have indicated their willingness to move towards active partnership. This is most welcome. The previous example shows how successful this can be. However, western governments have become very inwardly focused because of the financial crisis. It is not

easy to establish good relations with a government if you are dealing with people who do not know if they will have the same job in three months time, who do not know if they will continue in employment in the organisation, or who are new and inexperienced in their work. Green Square awaits decisions about internal reorganisation. If governments want to be effective and active partners, they should remain outward looking and connected.

Finally: *Enterprise*

It is time to give, share and create. It will pay to be vulnerable here. Look for suitable alliances, not just in the private sector. Broad cooperative links offer new openings and perspectives in business, and increase the chance of success. Working with the Green Square method offers an opportunity to become stronger. It is of course part of the natural process for people to become more attuned to each other. It is therefore a great challenge to achieve constructive collaboration. We cannot be successful without our Green Square partnership. Time will tell.

Concluding remarks

This chapter has allowed us to show you how GreenDreamCompany applies the African philosophy of Ubuntu. We have only touched on its possibilities. There are many variations and ways of thinking, depending on the circumstances of the organisation or company, and the objectives they are striving for. It would be easier to integrate this philosophy into the work place from the start of implementing a new business. We found ourselves in fortunate circumstances. But it is certainly possible to apply Ubuntu within an existing situation. Look for space. Recommendations based on our experience show that there is a world yet to be conquered.

This requires leaders who want something different not to let go of their ambitions and good intentions, or to stand looking admiringly on from the sidelines. They must be able to strike out from the field and make progress. Tomorrow, or even today.

Our journey has only just started; perhaps yours has also begun...

Epilogue

What is your role? What are you going to do?

The process of change on the world stage is clearly visible to everyone. An irreversible movement demanding participation is happening on a personal level, in a personal context and in the work place. This process affects us all, in every position.

The choice remains now: what is your position and what are you going to do?

Who are you? What is your view of life and vision of people? How do you carry out Ubuntu in your immediate surroundings? Your household? Your family? Your friends? Will you immerse yourself and connect with tribal communities who help to strengthen your feelings and identity effectively enough to give your own happiness a helping hand? These tribal communities make themselves heard via social media and the Internet, and are very accessible.

Does it suit you to be a tribal team member? Do you feel at home in a multicultural team? How global are you and your team? Do you know what drives your colleagues, and what their unique selling points are? Do you make good use of the global character? Your team's opportunities can increase enormously and your work becomes more pleasant. You can become a world team.

Or are you the diaspora, bridging several cultures? You hold a key role in this transition phase. How can you make yourself seen and heard, and at the same time be as important for your fatherland as your mother country? As team member, tribal leader and human being, you could invest in joint opportunities and concerns.

Perhaps you are self-employed or work alone, and you think cooperation is a good idea in this complex time. You may or may not wish to retain your independence, so you could connect with any of the existing variations of collaboration, or join a self-employed or collective work place where your colleagues meet each other.

Do you work in the government, education or care services? Take a look at people oriented concepts. Do you work in jurisprudence? Perhaps you have ideas about how to incorporate forgiveness and shame into the western blame culture. Mediation is always a good starting point. The power of the word 'sorry' in the mediation process offers to both offender and victim an opening to be seen as real people.

'If it comes to talking about the future, there are three sorts of people: those who let it happen, those who shape it and those who wonder what it's all about.'

John M. Richardson

But perhaps you are a tribal leader of the future. The world needs innovative spirits to face, approach and shape the global challenges ahead of us. Do you know how to connect and inspire people? It is time for the next step: find the human power behind the professional. Recovery requires good advisors, and possibly tapping into whole new markets.

> *'Don't say you don't have enough time. You have exactly the same number of hours in per day that were given to Helen Keller, Pasteur, Michelangelo, Mother Teresa, Leonardo da Vinci, Thomas Jefferson and Albert Einstein.'*
> **H. Jackson Brown Jr. (1940)**

This is a time for reappraisal. There has never been a better moment. Do not say that you do not have enough time.

How will you connect to this new transition phase? Where will you stand in this new world ten years from now?

This is an enthralling time.

If I had my life to live over
I'd dare to make more mistakes next time
I'd relax, I'd limber up.
I would be sillier than I have been this trip
I would take fewer things seriously
I would take more chances.

I would climb more mountains and swim more rivers
I would eat more ice cream and less beans.
I would perhaps have more actual troubles,
But I'd have fewer imaginary ones.

You see, I'm one of those people who live
Sensibly and sanely hour after hour
Day after day.

Oh' I've had my moments
And if I had to do it over again,
I'd have more of them.
In fact, I'd try to have nothing else.
Just moments, one after another,
Instead of living so many years ahead of each day.

I've been one of those people who never goes anywhere
Without a thermometer, a hot water bottle, a raincoat
And a parachute.
If I had to do it again, I would travel lighter than I have.

If I had my life to live over,
I would start barefoot earlier in the spring
And stay that way later in the fall.
I would go to more dances.
I would ride more merry-go-rounds.
I would pick more daisies.

Nadine Stair, 85 years old

Sources of Inspiration

Bibliography

Bakas, Adjiedj, *World Megatrends*, Scriptum, Schiedam, 2011.

Battle, Michael, *Reconciliation: The Ubuntu Theology Of Desmond Tutu*, Pilgrim Press, Cleveland, 2009.

Godin, Seth, *Tribes: Jij moet ons leiden*, A.W. Bruna Uitgevers, Utrecht, 2009.

Jonker, Jan, *Duurzaam Denken Doen, 2011-2035: Inspiratieboek Voor Onze Gezamenlijke Toekomst*, Kluwer, Deventer, 2012.

Jonker, Jan i.s.m. Marloes Tap en Tim van Straten, *Nieuwe Business Modellen: Een exploratief onderzoek naar veranderende transacties die meervoudige waarde creëren*, paper Radboud Universiteit Nijmegen, 2012.

Kitzen, Monique, 'Gewoon Charisma'. *Quest*, mei 2005.

Liefde, Willem de, *African tribal leadership voor managers*, Kluwer, Deventer, 2007.

Lundin, Stephen en Bob Nelson, *Ubuntu! Een inspirerend verhaal over de Afrikaanse traditie van teamwork en samenwerking*, Mouria, Baarn, 2012.

Maffesoli, Michel, *The Time of the Tribes: The Decline of Individualism in Mass Society*, Sage, Londen, 1996.

Malunga, Chiku, *Understanding Organizational Leadership Through Ubuntu*, Adonis & Abbey Publishers, Londen, 2009.

Mbigi, Lovemore, *The Spirit of African Leadership*, Knowres, Randburg, 2005.

Shirky, Clay, *Here Comes Everybody: How Change Happens When People Come Together*, Penguin Books, Londen, 2009.

Weggeman, Mathieu, *Leidinggeven aan professionals? Niet doen!*, Scriptum, Schiedam, 2008.

Websites

www.acta.nl
www. africanews.com
www.africaopenforbusiness.com
www.diaspora-centre.org
www.economist.com
www.emergingafrica.nl
www.greendreamcompany.com
www.grotewoorden. tctubantia.nl
www.harrybijl.nl
www.ikbenomdatwijzijn.info
www.janklerk.net
ww.nabc.nl
www.nuzakelijk.nl
www.sethgodin.com
www.sinarwanda.com
www.ted.com
www.thinkerstop50.com
www.ubuntu.com
www.ubuntucircle.nl
www.unwto.org
www.vno-ncw.nl
www.wetenschap.infonu.nl

Strength

Adaptability

Energy

Freedom
& Emancipation

Supremacy
of God

Harmony

Intelligence

Power of Love

Peace

Transformation

Unity in
Diversity

Universe

Adrinka Symbols

Adrinka symbols are visual symbols which illustrate the concept of aphorism. They originate from the Akan in Ghana and the Gyaman of the Ivory Coast of West Africa. Adrinka symbols are used on fabric, walls, pottery, woodcarvings and logos. They can also be used to convey messages in everyday life. There are many different symbols, each with a unique pattern and meaning.

Appendix

Farewell speech by Liepollo l. Pheko

Farewell speech for CIDA City Campus students, by Liepollo l. Pheko, 2010

Dear Programme Director, Chancellor, Acting Dean, Board Chair and Board members, distinguished guests, lecturers, academic faculty, CIDA community, parents and mostly the wonderful young people and graduating class – all protocols are observed. It's a great honour and I thank you for the invitation and opportunity to speak today and in some way contribute to your onward journey.

Ralph Waldo Emerson once asked **what we would do if the stars only came out once every thousand years.** Of course none of us would sleep that night. The world would become instantly religious and be overcome by the awesome power of creation and the glory of the Creator. We would be ecstatic, delirious, made rapturous by the glory of God. Instead the stars come out every night, and we watch television, check out Facebook, YouTube and Twitter. We barely even go jogging or visit the gym in lieu of watching the miracle that is the stars.

I once read a quote which said: **'If you live each day as if it was your last, someday you'll most certainly be right.'** It made an impression on me. And since then, for the past years, I have looked in the mirror every morning and asked myself: 'If today were the last day of my life, would I still want to do what I am about to do today?' And whenever the answer has been 'No' for too many days in a row, we know we must change something. This day is not a given. It holds no guarantees and deserves to be treated with that understanding. As you walk the path you've chosen, remember that the road ahead is paved with relationships. We've all enjoyed some great fortune, but none of it would have happened without the people who shared their wisdom, the hard work of people, professionals, artisans, artists, teachers, community leaders worldwide, and the love and support of family and friends. It might even have been a taxi or bus driver, a spaza owner on our street, a cleaner at our school who constantly encouraged you. **Remember ... there's no such thing as a self-made success. Motho ke motho ka batho.**

Young people are doing amazing things around the world and throughout history. One of my favourites is David, who volunteered to slay the Giant Goliath. He ran up to the giant and as Goliath laughed in derision ... he struck the giant dead. Each of us has our many many Goliaths to slay in this life. Others are the many people who through-out history have led revolutions and shifted the course of lives in tangible and intangible ways. These can be the children and youths of the 1976 June 16th uprising, the youths in China who marched to Tiananmen Square to demand citizenship rights on June 4, 1989. They seized their today with valour and urgency. Often courage emerges almost incidentally from these very conditions. It can be the young people blessed with talent and opportunities to play sports very well, such as the sisters Venus and Serena Williams, or sing before huge audiences, like the late and great Michael Jackson. The roll call of honour also includes the youth who raise their own siblings, who walk many miles to and from school or who persevere with no tangible means of support or visible reason to hope for anything different. They walk step-by-step journeys of miles maybe understanding the saying: 'that neither flying nor walking on water are miracles. No – the miracle is in walking on this earth, in this reality daily.' I add that daring to dream is part of lifting our feet as we walk or trudge and putting those dreams in action is what lifts us indeed to the dizzy heights.

Deserve before you desire. Character is the best of legacies and what others will say when we die is one motivator to build good character while we live. With the desire to be great, to achieve, to transform, to revolutionise, to be famous, to be wealthy and to have power comes immense responsibility. This requires the ability, capacity and strength to stand firmly on one's principals, to practice decency. Decency is a much underrated attribute and a much needed antidote to the selfish, corrupt and thoughtless behaviour which often arrives a moment after our success and accolades. To deserve is to continuously and consciously provide good

ground for God to plant blessings into our lives and know that these will be treat-
ed with reverence. To deserve is to realise the stakes of non-conformity and stand by them. To deserve is to wish others at least what we wish for ourselves. Ambition is good fuel for the journey but is pointless unless a good legacy is the ultimate destination. Integrity, decency, kindness, diligence, passion, generosity, wisdom, perseverance, focus... only some aspects of character and the building blocks of legacy.

Play to win but **win with fairness**. Where opportunity does not present itself or offer introductions do not trick it, force it or cheat it into being. It will not often nor is it obliged to come up and introduce itself to us. Most often it is the combination of planning, positioning and focus which open us to opportunity. Do not steal, envy or begrudge anybody else's opportunity. Where opportunity does not knock, build a door of your own and walk through it.

Enjoy whatever you do. Sir Thomas Lipton is credited with the statement, 'There is no greater fun than hard work'. You usually excel in fields which you truly enjoy. **Passion, passion, passion.** Ask any person what it is that inter-
feres with their enjoyment of existence. They will say that it is their boring job, dull social life, unhappy family life, difficult living environment or hours of commuting. That, frankly, life is no fun.

Find allies rather than adorers. You can choose to surround yourself with adorers who are easy to be around but never tell you when you mess up. Instead, seek out allies who are honest with you when they know you are not living up to your potential; people who challenge you to be the best you can be.

We do not always have to be the most clever or loudest or have the best singing voice in the room. And if by chance we are, it is advisable to invite smarter people or those with lovelier voices… or find a different room. In professional circles it is called networking. In organisations it's called team building. And in life it is called family, friends and community. We are all gifts to each other, and my own growth as a leader has shown me again and again that the most rewarding experiences come from my **relationship**s. And it sure keeps me humble and keeps my singing voice in perspective. Direction is more important than distance. Go confidently in the direction of your dreams and live the life you have imagined. It requires pace and grace more than speed and greed. It is often all we can do and perhaps is frankly all we should do.

We are living in very strange times. We are living in sometimes scary times. In all this we must consider the terror of the real wars. The war against poverty, the terror of hunger, the terror of being orphaned by AIDS. The war against hope. The war against audacity. The war against knowledge and access to the truths it can tell us. The tyranny against ideas and innovation. The attempt to turn us into carbon copies of each other. These are the true weapons of mass destruction.

What is the space for youth citizenship in the midst of this? How do these circumstances and challenges galvanise youth participation and leadership in creating a new and better reality across nations and sectors? What is the purpose of citizenship for the widow, the orphan, the landless, the disabled, for women, or for people of colour and youths? For those who are disinterested in politics and disappointed by politicians? How do these link with the struggles for goodness, greatness and decency in every sphere of life including business, family, media, culture, sports and yes – politics?

The value depends on the narrative that you are leaving this institution to create. The value of life is equal to the value we give it. It is a mirror of ourselves. That it is why all these things and many more are worth knowing about, worth thinking about, worth caring about and worth fighting for. There is quote which says human life is purely a matter of deciding what is important to you.

In valuing life we value self, each other and this earth. We recognise the deficits and opportunities of being alive on this earth today. We recognise the imbalances between the north and south, between women and men, between black and white people, between elders and youths.

We dare to interrupt the ridiculous conversations which have reached preposterous conclusions about us. When we value self we decide that not having trust funds or famous surnames or connections will deter us. In fact we celebrate the path that is less travelled and replete with new possibilities.

The generation I come from will never be twenty years old again. When you wonderful young people are older, you can and should be different from my generation. Ours is a great and wonderful continent, and realising her true potential in the global arena depends ever so much on the quality and persistence of our young people. **You should in other words go further than I or any of the many brilliant people assembled here today**.

This astonishing moment when we are globally aware of each other and the collective dangers that threaten all civilisation has never happened, not in a thousand years, not in ten thousand years. **Each of us is as complex and beautiful as all the stars in the universe. Each of us in fact is one of those stars designed to shine, energise, lead and create a particular corner of history. Each of us is the author of our own story and in fact a piece of history which will not be written unless we are ready to take the mantle.** Humanity has done great things and but has often gone amiss in terms of honouring creation.

You are graduating to the most amazing, demanding, stupefying challenge ever bequeathed to any generation. The generations before you failed in some respects. We didn't stay up all night watching the stars. We sometimes got distracted and lost sight of the fact that life is a miracle every moment of existence. Nature beckons you to be on her side. You could not ask for a better boss. **The most un-realistic person in the world is the cynic, not the dreamer**. Hopefulness only makes sense when it doesn't make sense to be hopeful. This is your century. This is your time. This is your moment. There will never be another like it. Take it and run as if your life depends on it. While Goliath is unaware, unbelieving, unconvinced or unimpressed by your abilities, strike him down. There is nothing to lose. There is no shame in endeavour. The stakes are high, the rewards are higher and the legacy immense. Behave as audaciously and urgently as though the stars have come out for the first time in a thousand years. **Dare... this is the moment**. I salute you graduates.

About the author

Leontine S.A.A. van Hooft (1959) was born in Maasdriel, The Netherlands. She grew up among the woodlands and fens of Oisterwijk, which still influences her work. After her studies, she moved to the attractive fortified town of Zaltbommel, on the river Waal.

As an independent organisational advisor, Leontine has guided both goverments and enterprises in the area of cultural change. She specialises in managing diversity and integrity, and cross-cultural communication. At the age of 45, she embarked on her Masters Degree in organisational anthropology at the University of Utrecht, The Netherlands.

Leontine is the co-founder and owner of GreenDreamCompany. This company specialises in the realisation of sustainable tourist development centres in emerging African countries, based on the five P's: People, Planet, Profit, Pleasure and Passion. The company was founded on Ubuntu values.

Through lectures, workshops and forums, Leontine conveys her vision of entrepreneurs incorporating Ubuntu as a philosophy in organisational development.

She received the regional award of Woman of the Year in 2011, for her inspiring entrepreneurship.

More information:
Leontine van Hooft
leontinevanhooft@gmail.com
l.van.hooft@greendreamcompany.com
Twitter @ubuntu_for_you @leontinevhooft
www.leontinevanhooft.nl
www.greendreamcompany.com

Printed in Great Britain
by Amazon

82690945R00060